Withlacoochee Notes :

A History of the Land Along the River From

the Gulf, Through Levy and into Marion County

By: Arnold Dix Stephens

PO Box 2125
Trenton, Florida 32693
dix1034@yahoo.com

Library of Congress No.

Additional copies of this publication may be purchased from the author or the publisher at:

WWW.Lulu.com/content/202788

Prologue

1836
Fort Smith, Arkansas Territory

It is said that in death, all things become clear. The Indian woman now knew it was true. As she clutched her daughter to her side, she felt the life-force slowly flowing out of both their bodies. Silently she prayed to the Great Spirit to receive them into his realm.

Foke-Luste-Hajo, or Black Dirt as he was called by the white man, looked on. He had done all the white man had demanded of him, even more. He had known it would be difficult to begin anew in a strange land but now he would be truly alone.

Introduction

Planning an orchard was extremely exacting work for our ancestors. In the 1700s the apple was our national food and cider was the national drink. By the 1800s in Florida, citrus, which had been cultivated by the Indians, was discovered by the white settlers. The first colonists in this country had been instructed to drink as little water as possible. They had obeyed this dictum so well that even small children were brought up on teas and beers, and cider was served at every meal. Orchards were planted such that different varieties of fruit would be bearing at differing times. By proper planning and hastening or retarding ripening, an orchard might start its harvest period in summer and finish well into winter.

Scratching the bark of a fruit tree at certain times will hasten its bloom, and it was even a custom to shoot buckshot at an apple tree to help it bear in an "off year". Beating a tree's bark will bruise the layer just beneath it and check the descent of sap, forcing an early bearing. People used to beat fruit and nut trees with softwood clubs, and an old rhyme mentions this:

> *A woman, a watchdog, and a walnut tree,*
> *The more you beat them the better they be.*

I remember my father in the 1950s being able to get fruit trees to bear by "shocking" them as he would say; and he didn't need to consult the *Farmers' Almanac* as the information necessary to produce a crop was well known to him through experience. In the early twentieth century produce from the family garden was a necessity and might mean the difference in whether you ate or went hungry. Dad saved the seeds from better fruits and vegetables for his garden the following year. Today few people grow the things they eat and those that try usually purchase young plants some professional grower has started. If they are brave and use seed, the only ones for sale produce hybrid plants that don't produce viable seeds so you must purchase seeds again in following years. While it is very convenient to simply visit the nearest grocery store many people today don't know where their foods are coming from (or what country in the world) and children don't understand the milk in their cereal came originally from a cow rather than a plastic carton.

In my short span of sixty one years I have been witness to many changes. Young people and the ever increasing population of "new people" to our area are not aware of our history and "how and why we do things" or why some things are named or called what they are. Realizing the lack of written records on the history of this area and learning that some of the few things written are inaccurate, I wish to set this right by producing this manuscript.

I do not claim it to be thorough or to contain all that perhaps it could, simply that it includes most of what is important as to how we came to "be here" and that it is as absolutely correct as it was possible for me to make it. I have boldly stated that some previously told stories are fiction, but I give references and proof for these statements, recognizing that some future writer may wish to correct my work.....and that is acceptable if the proof is given.

Finally, let me say that history is important. It is only by understanding who we are and where we have been that we can set a course into our future.

Table of Contents

Illustrations:

In the beginning

The area of North America known today as Florida rose from the ocean and descended again beneath the waters time after time over the eons leaving various ridges, many still visible today, which at one time were the shorelines. By the time of the first Europeans arrival in the new world, Florida was well populated by several different Indian cultures.

The Timucua lived in the area that would become Levy County, with their primary village Ocali in what is now Marion County, and from which Ocala takes its name. Hunter-gatherers, they lived near reliable food sources and fresh water. They grew some crops including corn, squash and beans but also went to the coast in the fall when the fish came inshore and up the creeks. Here they would dine on fish and shellfish, leaving accretal mounds (meaning that burial and religious mounds were often located on top of an ordinary midden mound). Most of these mounds have been lost to history as their contents were used by early road builders.

Timcuan village. Photo courtesy of Florida State Archives, Photo collection.

The Timucua were composed of several tribes which shared a common language but despite their commonalities, they were hostile to one another. This hostility and subsequent warring among themselves, combined with the diseases and conflict with the Spaniards and the slave practices of the Europeans, the numbers of these aboriginal people were severely depleted by the late 1600s. Even the common cold was disastrous for the Indians, but also they were exposed to influenza and smallpox.

Attack on the Timucuans by the Spanish. Photo courtesy of the Florida State Archives Photo collection.

Even before the Revolutionary War there was increasing pressure on the indigenous population by the Colonists, additionally there was warfare between these Indians. The Seminoles, considered runaways themselves, were of various ethnic, political, and linguistic backgrounds. These Indians evolved as an identifiable group after they migrated to Florida and absorbed the remnants of Indian tribes there. As early as the late 1700s, the English had begun calling them Seminoles, from the Muskogee (Creek) word *simanoli*, meaning runaway or wild. The Seminoles who migrated to Florida in the 1700 and 1800s were generally from the Upper and Lower Creek towns that spread over Georgia and Alabama. Of course the Creek nation itself was a melting pot of different ethnic groups. The Seminoles filled a vacuum that had been created by the near annihilation of Florida's aboriginal population. The Spanish even encouraged Indians from the Lower Creek towns to occupy land along the border of Florida and Georgia to create a buffer zone between Spanish Florida and the advancing Colonial settlements.

Following the Revolutionary War, when Spain regained control of Florida from Britain, Spanish colonists and settlers from the newly formed United States poured into Florida, many being lured by the promise of land grants. Instead of becoming more Spanish, Florida instead became more "American". Additional pressure was experienced by the increasing number of slaves slipping into Florida and the safe-haven provided by the Seminoles. Georgia was particularly concerned as that State experienced incursion across the border when Indians would attack settlements, running off stock and slaves.

In November, 1817, a military conflict erupted when General Edmund Gaines attempted to take Chief Neamathla into custody. The fighting that ensued is considered the start of the First Seminole War. Four months later, President Monroe sent General Andrew Jackson into the mess. Monroe suspected Jackson could seize Florida if given the chance. General Jackson, with 3,500 men, half of them Creek Warriors, invaded West Florida. In just eleven weeks, from March 9 to May 24, 1818, he had destroyed Indian settlements and their fighting strength west of the Suwannee River. He also captured the two Spanish settlements of St. Marks and Pensacola. This foray into Florida ended the First Seminole War and convinced the Spanish that she had lost control of the Territory.

An 1821 engraved portrait of Florida's first Territorial Governor General Andrew Jackson. He served as Governor of East and West Florida from March 10 until December 31, 1821. Photo courtesy of Florida State Archives Photo collection.

Spain eventually would cede the Florida Territory to the United States in 1819 for the sum of $ 5,000,000, although we didn't actually take possession until 1821. The territory was divided into East and West Florida (much as the Spanish had done) and two counties were created: Escambia and St. Johns with the dividing line being the Suwannee River. Andrew Jackson, who had largely contributed to the "mess" with Spain, was rewarded by being named the first Territorial Governor.

From the very beginning, the United States felt the only "good" Indian was a dead Indian....or at the very least a "good" Indian was one that moved out of the way of "progress". The United States immediately began encouraging the Indians to relocate further West to what would become known as Indian Territory, in what is now Oklahoma. Some Indian leaders even signed a treaty in 1832 agreeing to move "in a few years" and in the meantime restricting their activities to a reservation.

During the wars with the Indians, the United States practiced a "scorched earth" policy of destruction. In the long history of man's inhumanity to man, racial conflict of this type has produced some of the most horrible examples of brutality.

When Indians went to war and killed, it was always referred to as a massacre; however, when the white men burned whole Indian towns and killed the inhabitants, it was generally always justified as military strategy.

Most Seminoles did not recognize the treaty and when the U. S. Army arrived in 1835 to enforce it, many Indians were ready for combat; this led to the Second Seminole War of 1835-1842.

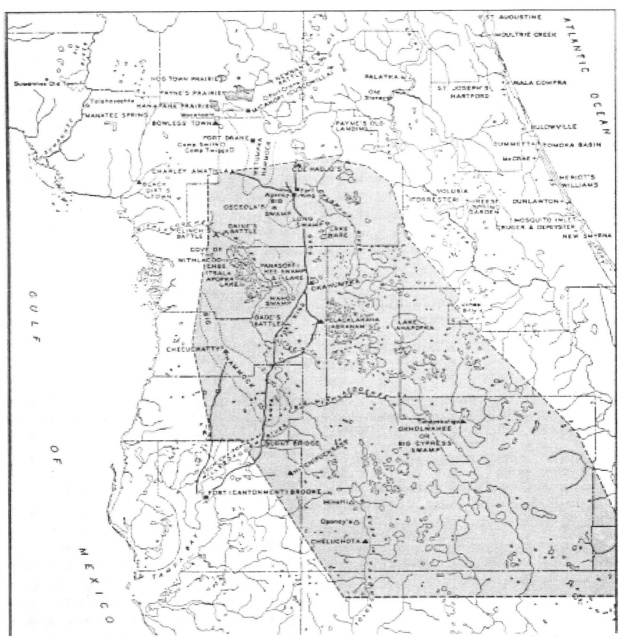

The above map shows the initial reservation boundary which extended from Fort King in the north (near present day Ocala) to just below Tampa Bay. Notice how the Seminoles were restricted to the center of the state.

In a curious footnote to history, Seminole Chief Osceola warned Brigadier General Duncan L. Clinch in February 1836. Osceola told the General,

"...you have men, and so have we, you have powder and lead, and so have we, your men will fight, and so will ours, till the last drop of.....blood has moistened the dust.....".

General Duncan L. Clinch who owned "Auld Lang Syne", a sugar plantation ten miles south of Micanopy. In charge of U.S. troops in Florida he led 250 regulars and 500 Florida volunteers against the Seminoles in a battle by the Withlacoochee River, December 31, 1835. Photo courtesy Florida State Archives photo collection.

From a lithograph of Seminole Chief Osceola by George Catlin in 1837 courtesy of Florida State Archives photo collection.

An exception was Foke-Luste-Hajo, called Black Dirt, who was a Seminole Chief who recognized the folly of continued resistance and even assisted the U.S. Army early in the Second Seminole War (see Report Books of Office of Indian Affairs, Annual Reports 1832-1842, National Archives, Washington, D. C., Microfilm 348). Before being forced to move onto the reservation following the First Seminole War, his tribe had resided in what is now Levy County.

Close by, also in Levy County, had been the residence of another Seminole Chief, Charley Amathla. Amathla (sometimes spelled Emathla or Emarthla) was killed in 1835 by supporters of Osceola who were anti-removal. Shortly after Amathla's death, Black Dirt encouraged his followers to accept removal to the West.

Foke-Luste-Hajo, or Black Dirt as the whiteman called him. Photo courtesy of The Great Seminole Nation of Okalahoma.

From Jane F. Lancaster's *Removal Aftershock: the Seminoles' struggles to survive in the West,* page 20-21, we read:

"Several months passed before the arrival of the first group of Florida Indians in Indian Territory. This party of friendly Seminoles, led by Chiefs Holati Emathla and Foke-Luste-Hajo (Black Dirt) and supervised by Lieutenant Joseph W. Harris, who escorted it from Florida via New Orleans, reached Little Rock, Arkansas, on 5 May 1836. When Harris described these Indians to Secretary of War Lewis Cass in July 1836, he said they had been reduced to a wretched condition in Florida. Hated and despised by their fellow countrymen for not resisting removal, they had lost everything. For more than a year, most of them had wandered about after having their cabins and other property destroyed by their brethren. Exposure, fatigue, privation, and persecution reduced their numbers and made their condition wretched.

After their arrival at Little Rock, these Seminoles faced an additional month of misery and agony. They disembarked from their steamboat at McLain's Bottom on 9 May. Lieutenant J. Van Horne took the group with a few wagons of Indian goods –

blankets, shirts, corn, bacon, other treaty provisions, and about twenty horses they had bought – to Seminole country, a distance of 127 miles. A severe outbreak of measles had spread from twenty to seventy-eight of them between 9 and 13 May. The accompanying doctor feared the epidemic would attack them all, because the Indians refused his prescriptions, bathed in the cold river water, and camped in filthy surroundings....He kept a daily journal in which he described hardships the Indians endured: the constant rain, lack of roads, flies, sickness and death. On 15 and 16 May, Van Horne reported that he had on his hands from 130 to 150 sick Indians. Some were placed in wagons; others too sick to travel were left behind to die. Ten days later, after continuous rain, the whole country was a quagmire, and each wagon had to be dragged by ten or twelve yoke of oxen. The rain soaked the exhausted Indians, and under these conditions the disease spread. By 28 May, at least twenty Indians lay dying in their own filth; the odor tainted the air in the camps. From one to four died daily."

Photo courtesy Florida State Archives photo collection.

They eventually reached the Little River about 90 miles Southwest of Fort Gibson on land assigned their tribe but the Creeks indiscriminately occupied the best parts of these lands. Subsequently when the Seminole emigrants arrived, they found their country already occupied. The trip was arduous and Black Dirt's efforts were rewarded when his wife and daughter died on the way!

Forts, called Blockhouses, were constructed throughout the territory. Logs were placed upright in trenches in a square pattern. One small doorway allowed access and gun ports located high in the walls afforded troops inside a manner to fire on any attacking savages. The roof was constructed of brush and palm fronds over logs. One such blockhouse was located on the north bank of the Withlacoochee River, a few miles from the mouth (in present day Yankeetown).

Known in history as Holloman's Blockhouse, its story is instructive and the following newspaper article transcribed from the *MONTGOMERY DEMOCRAT* of 13 July 1836:

"The Block House of the Withlacoochee.

The following interesting letter is the only authentic account, yet published, of the heroic defense of the Block House on the Withlacoochee, by Captain Hollman's (sic) command, and of the gallant relief of that party by the volunteers under Major Reed. It will be seen that under the greatest disadvantage and sufferings, thirty-eight men held the post, for two months, against the impetuous attacks of an overwhelming force of savages. It is not surprising that these heroes are every where received with all the honors that can be shown them. At Tallahassee, at Monticello, and wherever they have been they have been received in triumph, and their brave fellow citizens have vied with each other in doing honor to the brave.

Extract of a letter from Florida, published in the *Globe:*

The mind of the little public here is much occupied with Maj. Reed's expedition to the Withlacoochee. Both the Major and the Governor deserve great credit for relieving forty unfortunate men from a very perilous situation. You know that Major McLemore (now dead) commanded a party to the Withlacoochee for establishing a Depot, which, it was supposed, would be serviceable to General Scott's army. A block house was built near a lime sink containing water and communicating with the river. Provisions were deposited, and Capt. Hollman (sic) was left, with forty-five men, in command. The distance from the block house to the river was about fifteen yards. By some unaccountable _____ the party was abandoned or overlooked when the army retreated, and were often assailed by the Indians. McLemore, when left them, promised to return in ten days but these passed away and many more, and yet they were without news of the army or assistance from their friends. The Indians attacked them nearly every fifth day; sometimes they laughed at them, taunted them, ridiculed the army, bade them "come to the river and wash your feet", and in directing their fire at the block house, sometimes deridingly cried out –"' Eyes-right! Eyes-left! Port holes, shoot!" On several occasions *silver bullets* were fired from the Indians rifles, and with combustibles attached to arrows, they contrived to set the top of the block house on fire. The besieged threw off their roof, and then suffered much from exposure to the weather. Yet was there happily no sickness among them, and though the sides of the building were riddled by the shot of the enemy, none were killed or wounded within. Poor Hollman (sic) became, it is said, deranged, or at least partially so; his responsibility was felt too severely, and his mind was at times unsettled. He left the block house with a few men, for the purpose of procuring some timber with which to improve his fortification; and was killed, with several others, in a sudden and unexpected attack from the savages.

After his death the utmost harmony and good discipline prevailed. A simple military code was adopted by which every man was obliged to perform his duty, and especially to be vigilant. Its rigorous enforcement saved the party from surprise and death. One of the regulations required no musket to be fired unless the object was within reach and the aim sure. Many Indians were consequently killed, until at length they, taught by experience, maintained a more cautious distance. Another of their rules required a few persons to supervise those who were on guard, and to shoot down, without hesitation, him who did not strictly perform the duties of his watch. Minor punishments were prescribed, and, it is said, inflicted on all, for lower offences. At length the provisions were exhausted or spoiled, and the corn scarcely fit to eat. They resolved to send three of their number to seek for aid. The selection was by lot; the three solemnly promised to return as soon as possible if they were living men, and to cry aloud on their return within earshot, "alls' well". They embarked in a canoe perforated with bullets, at midnight, and made their way to the mouth of the river, and thence along the coast to St. Marks. Their course down the river was one of difficulty and peril. They feared to use their paddles or to bail the boat, which was half full of water, lest they should be heard by the savages on the bank when at sea. Their situation was little envied, for the boat could scarcely be kept above water. From St. Marks they came immediately hither, and when the Governor persuaded one of them to visit his family while the expedition for the relief of his comrades was preparing, he declined, saying he had promised to think only of the relief of his suffering friends, and he would not taste of the comforts of his house until that was accomplished. In a few days Maj. Reed, with eighty men, embarked in a steamboat at St. Marks. As the boat could not pass the bar at the mouth of the Withlacoochee, a lighter was prepared but she soon sunk. The steamboat put back, and a long barge and a quantity of lumber was procured. During the voyage the men fitted bulwarks and other defenses to the barge. The mouth of the river obtained, the barge proceeded up the river as noiseless as possible; but the moon was shining brightly, and the fires of the Indians were seen on the banks; they encountered a single obstacle – a log in the stream—it was soon cut away, and they proceeded. The party in the block house were, on that night, very desponding and they had determined, if aid did not arrive before the coming Saturday, to leave their prison and attempt to make their way to Camp King. When the noise of the approaching barge was first heard, it was supposed that the Indians were coming on in force to a night attack, but soon after the signal word, "all's well" was heard. A deep silence prevailed in the block house and for _____ not a word was uttered, -- then came the shout of joy, a long, loud hoorah – and loudly was it answered from the barge. Major Reed was soon near enough to make the proper inquiries, and give the necessary orders. The parties met – there was not a dry eye – tears flowed plenteously – and the deliverers were embraced by the delivered. I have not seen those details in print, I obtained them from one on the spot. The published reports are singularly unhappy."

"Attack of the Seminoles on the blockhouse", a lithograph of events in the Withlacoochee Battle in 1835 by T. R. Gray and James of Charleston, S.C., in 1837. Courtesy of Florida State Archives photo collection.

In an issue of the *Appalachicola Gazette* in November 1836, we read:

"The U. S. Steamer General Izard, in attempting to ascend the Wythlacoochee (sic) with supplies for the depot, got aground at the mouth of the river, with her bows on the bank on one side, and her stern on the other, and 8 feet of water in the middle of the channel. In this awkward position they remained till the tide went out when her centre timber gave way and she broke down...."

The Second Seminole Indian War was probably the fiercest war fought by the United States against the Native Americans and extremely costly both in funds and lives. The U. S. spent some $20 million, at least 1,500 military dead and an unknown number of settlers.

The following is a transcription by the author of an eyewitness account by an anonymous person in Levy County written in the early 1900s.

THE TWO IMPORTANT FORTS OF LEVY COUNTY IN INDIAN TIMES

Fort Jennings is located in Section 29, township 13, range 16; on the Waccassassee(sic) River, about three miles south east of Otter Creek. It was one of the line of Forts that was erected by General Jackson on the west coast in his effort to corral the Seminole Indians. This road through this county is known as the, "Old Jackson Trail", and connected the forts of Fannin in Alachua County and Jennings in Levy County. Fort Jennings was built about 1836 and was occupied by the U.S. Soldiers for several months. Later the detachment that was stationed there was moved further south and the fort was burned by the Indians. No record can be found of battles being fought at this place in 1837. Owing to the fact that in 1897 there was an order issued that records of these and other later wars could not be used because they were fast becoming worn out, and it is impossible to get all information about this fort and its commanders.

Fort Daniels was situated in Levy County in Section 11, township 13, range 14. It was one of the important forts of this part. In the year 1856 Captain Enoch Daniels reported Indian signs between Rocky settlement and Cedar Keys. He was ordered to raise a company of men and investigate. This he did at once and built a fort by standing pine logs on end. All the families for miles around came there to live.

During the time of the erection of this fort Mr. Daniels, while scouting, met a party of Indians at what is now known as Sweetwater on the Cedar Key road, about section 23, township 13, range 14. He had a fight with them killing, as he claimed, three of them. Then he outran the others and reached the fort safely. The men of Levy County that composed this company were Lieut Enoch Daniels, Jeremiah Brown, S. Cowden, James G. Daniels, James W. Daniels, Lewis Daniels, William Gore, Hamilton Hudson, Samuel Hudson Jr., Samuel Hudson Sr., Garrett Hudson, James Hudson, E. D. Hogans, Jesup Hogans, Steven Hogans, William A. Hill, John R. Hatcher, O.H.P. Kirkland, Benjamin Lane, Alfred Mooney, Hugh Morrison, Jasper Newsom, Saunders Nobles, Isaac Osteen, James Starling, Benjamin Smith, Aaron Smith, Hamilton Smith, James H. Smith, William P. Smith, W. F. Smith, F. Stapleton, L.A. Walker, P.A. Walker, Lewis Wilkerson, Joseph Wilkerson, Willis Wilkerson, Granvill Worthington, Samuel Worthington, Robert Watterson.

This Company gave about six months service, scouting over the lands in Gulf Hammock. Here they found many Indian signs but failed to locate Indians. They were disbanded for a short time and then called together again to assist in fighting in the southern part of the state where there were (sic) much trouble with the Seminoles.

We cannot account for why the writer of the above story failed to mention the other important fort in Levy County. Fort Clinch had been established on the north bank of the Withlacoochee River some ten miles upstream from the mouth in October 1836. Originally called Reed's Depot (for Major Reed of Holloman's Blockhouse fame), it was renamed in honor of General Duncan Lamont Clinch. The fort was abandoned in May 1842 at the end of the war.

During the latter part of the Seminole resistance, every conceivable weapon and device was used by the military forces to round up and annihilate the remaining Indians hiding in the Everglades. When bribery, trickery and other attempts failed to get them to surrender, other means were employed to speed up their extermination. Bloodhounds were used but without success and rewards (bounty) of $200 were offered for each dead Indian. The United States would send its top four Army Generals against the Seminoles and each would leave Florida with his reputation diminished. The fourth of them, Major General Thomas S. Jesup, claiming treachery on the part of the Indians, began to capture their leaders any way he could. Most notorious was his seizure of Osceola under a flag of truce! He was imprisoned in Fort Moultrie, South Carolina where he died. Decades later his grave would be excavated and his bones placed on display for tourist.

The last two U.S. Commanders of the Second War, Walter Armistead and Williams Jenkins Worth, relied on small detachments guided by captured blacks and Indian prisoners to penetrate the Everglades and discover the Indian hideouts. There they destroyed what was left of Seminole subsistence. Band after band of the Seminoles, ragged, hungry and out of ammunition, finally surrendered.

In August 1842, the U.S. declared the action at an end. During the seven years of war, we had committed every regiment of our Army to the fight, with a loss of some 1,500 soldiers most of them from disease. Thirty thousand militia were involved, many of whom perished. In the end over 4,000 Seminoles were forcibly moved west to Indian Territory in present day Okalahoma at a cost of nearly $ 15,000 and the life of one soldier for every two Indians removed. Remaining in Florida were about 350 Seminoles, all living south of Lake Okeechobee.

To further stabilize the peace, immigration of more white settlers was encouraged by the Armed Immigration Act of 1842. Governor Keith Call had suggested that settlers should be encouraged to move into the territory several years prior. The Act called for awarding 160 acres to any family that would live and work the land, build a home and clear at least 5 acres. After 5 years of residence, they would be given title to the property. The Act was titled "Armed Occupation" because initially the government was to also provide the settlers weapons to defend their homesteads, this provision was never fulfilled. Settlers were able to select land, not already occupied by whites, south of a line running east and west just south of present day Gainesville.

In 1855 war broke out again when conflicts over land arose between white settlers and the few remaining Indians. From *Seminoles, Days of Long Ago*, by Kenneth W. Mulder, page 30-31, we read:

"The white man's insatiable greed for land was the cause of the so called Third Seminole War....Many touted the reservation, assigned the Indians, as being more fertile than the Valley of the Nile. Slave labor could be used to grow sugar cane and rice.....Wealthy plantation owners and cattlemen began to plan an attack. They had great influence in Tallahassee and bombarded Washington with new demands for the deportation or killing of every Seminole in the state."

December 7, 1855, an Army surveyor crew came across an Indian camp in the Big Cypress Swamp. They tore up the garden and vandalized the place. While this was going on, Chief Billy Bowlegs arrived, as it was his home. The white men treated him harshly and departed. A few days later Chief Bowlegs with a small band sneaked up on the Army camp and caught them by surprise. At least two soldiers were killed and several more wounded before they could make good their escape. The Indians continued to seek revenge for this slight and other past hardships caused by the white man by attacking settlers. The State Militia was called out and companies were formed to protect the citizens and "put the Indians in their place!

Chief Billy Bowlegs in 1852. Photo courtesy of Florida State Archives photo collection.

In 1857 the Secretary of War finally admitted that the Seminoles had proved impossible for a modern Army to conquer through warfare. Instead, the U.S. Government encouraged the Indians to move to Indian Territory by attractive inducements of money and goods.

Winston Stephens

Winston Stephens served in the Florida State Militia for the normal 6 month enlistment from July 1857 to January 1858, leaving his family and plantation on the banks of the St. Johns River near Welaka to fight the Seminoles in south Florida swamps. He enlisted with two brothers in Ocala then reported with them to Fort Brooke in present day Tampa. The Militia had no uniforms and provided their own weapons and horses if serving in a cavalry unit. Winston is the brother of the author's Great Grandfather.

On 1 May, 1858, Chief Billy Bowlegs accepted the government's offer at a conference in Fort Myers and the band was loaded on the Steamboat *Grey Cloud* on 4 May 1858, and sent to New Orleans and from there on to the Indian Territory. A few hold outs remained in the wilds of the Everglades, probably 200 or less. Finally in 1957 they received status from the government, so after 100 years are no longer considered renegades.

John C. Chambers

During the 1850s, several important Levy County Pioneers arrived in Florida. The first was John C. Chambers who came from York District,

South Carolina. His father was a large land owner and raised cotton as his primary money crop. In the fall of 1838, Samuel Chambers had taken ill and died leaving his wife with six minor children.

An abstract of the will of Samuel Chambers reads:

"....As the principal part of my estate consists of land & being desirous that my wife & children should always have a comfortable & decent support, my executors shall sell off whenever the necessities of my said wife and children may require such portions of my real estate. To my wife Elizabeth Chambers and my children William Elleson, Samuel C.C., Elizabeth J., John C., Benjamin, and Mary A. Chambers, all of my estate both real and personal in such portions as they will be entitled to under the statute of distribution of South Carolina, mainly one third to my said wife and the balance in equal portions to my children. I appoint my wife and my friends Benjamin Chambers and my oldest son Elleson Chambers when he comes of age, and also my son Samuel when he comes of age, executors, ___April 1838."

In 1850, John C. Chambers gave his occupation as merchant for the Federal Census and was living and working in Richland, S.C. He resided in a boarding house with several other businessmen. When he learned of the opportunities in Florida, he headed south and became a land-speculator and lumberman. Land could be acquired by homesteading which required living on and improving the land for a period of years (usually 5) or by outright purchase. With money in hand, John C. Chambers began land acquisitions in Putnam County in 1853. Eventually he would purchase hundreds of acres of land in Putnam, St. Johns, Marion and Levy Counties.

The 1860 census lists him living alone in the Long Pond District of Levy County. He was age 34, had been born in South Carolina and gave his profession as farmer. As far as we can tell, he never married. Quite wealthy for the time, his real estate was listed in the tax records of Levy County as valued at $25,000 and personal property valued at $73,100, yet in the 1860

Slave Schedule he is not listed, further confirming that he was not a farmer of crops but a lumberman and probably land speculator, thus no slaves.

A sawmill, run by water, had been built by Simpson & Company at Woodbine, near Pensacola about 1826. The first steam driven mill was built about 1841, also near Pensacola.

Early sawmill. Photo courtesy of the Florida State Archives photo collection.

As early as 1835 Pensacola exported some four million board-feet of lumber in eighty-five sailing ships. By 1850 the lumber business had expanded to some fourteen million board-feet. By 1855 many of the mills had shifted to steam power but the logging business mostly remained confined to the immediate vicinity of rivers so logs could be rafted to the mills. Logs were pulled to nearby waterways by oxen or mule teams and "high wheelers". Oxen were slower but with their large cloven hooves could manage in the soft ground of marshes and swamps better than mules.

The high wheeler allowed the front of the log to be raised slightly which made it slide more easily over the ground. Photo courtesy of Florida State Archives Photo Collection.

Typical log raft in Florida mid nineteenth to early twentieth century. Photo courtesy of Florida State Archives photo collection.

In 1860 Chambers acquired 300 acres "along Tenmile Creek" in Section 24, Township 15 Range 15 which was known as Chambers Field and a road by that name still exists in Gulf Hammock Wildlife Management Area. Important to us in Levy County is that Chambers constructed a large sawmill on an island at the mouth of the Withlacoochee River. This island would become known as Chambers Mill Point and later Chambers Island, even though Chambers never actually owned it! Logs would be cut as far away as Marion County and rafted down river to the mill.

Photo courtesy of the Florida State Archives Photo Collection.

Trees were first girdled as shown in the above photo. This caused them to dry out, making them much lighter. Then when cut they could more easily be handled or could be floated down river.

The virgin Florida forests contained trees of immense size like the cypress above. Wasteful logging practices and poor utilization caused depletion of these old growth trees. Photo courtesy of Florida State Archives photo collection.

The logs were cut into lumber which was then taken offshore to be loaded onboard ships for transport to markets.

The mouth of the Withlacoochee River being quite shallow most of the year, ocean going vessels were prohibited from approaching the sawmill on Chambers Island. Instead they would anchor some 5 miles off shore in the deepest water near the island. This place would become known as the Five Fathom Pool, it being near 30 feet in depth. Later, during the phosphate era, this pool would play an important part in our history once again. The photo on the next page is of a typical sailing ship used to transport lumber. During the phosphate shipping boom, these sailing ships actually would dock at Chambers Island during the high water periods on the river.

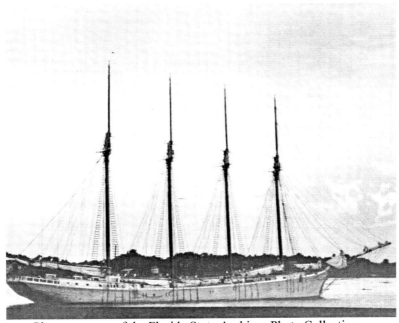

We know Chambers' sawmill was active prior to the Civil War. It has been reported that this sawmill was the largest one in operation on the west coast of Florida as late as 1870 but no reference for that statement was given and therefore can not be verified. The Citrus County Historical Society has suggested this sawmill was in operation as late as 1875 but no reference is given for that claim either. Sidney Lanier, at the time an unsuccessful poet, was hired by the Atlantic Coastline Railroad to write a handbook on Florida which they hoped to use to promote tourism and settlement. His book, *Florida: its Scenery, Climate and History* was published in 1875, perhaps this is where some of this confusion is derived for on page 101 we read, *"One of the largest sawmills in Florida is situated at the mouth of the Withlacoochee, and is supplied with material from the timber floated down that stream"*. Lanier did not actually visit every location he wrote about in his book and it does not appear from what he writes that he ever personally visited the Withlacoochee River. It would seem, therefore, that he "heard" about there having been a large sawmill in that location and included it in his writings, after all, accuracy was not a requirement, he was paid to write an interesting document that would encourage travelers to utilize the railroad to visit Florida.

We know that when Pensacola was abandoned by the Confederates in 1862, sawmills around the town were destroyed by order of General Bragg, to prevent their use by Federal Troops. This author has discovered no reports as to what happened to Chambers sawmill, but surely it would have been destroyed by either Confederate or Union troops if it had existed during the war, more likely it was dismantled by Chambers himself.

On 11 January 1862, Commander Goldsborough of the U.S. Navy reported to his commander at Key West his belief that the Confederate steamer, *Gladiator*, was planning to unload supplies at Cedar Key. According to his information the Confederate troops that had been located at Sea Horse Key had moved to some other position and as the place appeared abandoned, he recommended a small force be dispatched to destroy the railroad bridge which would prevent further movement of Confederate materials from the wharfs inland.

On 16 January 1862 the *USS Hatteras* arrived and landed Federal troops at Cedar Key and Sea Horse Key. Several guns and much ammunition were reported captured at the east end of Sea Horse. In Cedar Key they destroyed the railroad depot and wharf, several boxcars loaded with supplies, the telegraph office and a turpentine warehouse. Four schooners, three sloops, one ferry, a sailboat and a launch were captured. One Schooner, the *Stag*, which was loaded with naval stores and cotton was run ashore and set on fire by Federal gunfire. Another schooner, *Fanny*, was captured with a partial load of turpentine. Fifteen Confederates were captured.

The Confederate War Department demanded an accounting from Florida as to the disastrous attack on Cedar Key. General Trapier sent a report explaining that little resistance was attempted because it would have been hopeless and could only result in drawing fire from the Union vessels, causing useless destruction of private property and shedding of blood, perhaps the blood of women and children. The General reported that, contrary to reports, the Confederates did attempt escape by embarking a flat ferry scow, but when they reached midstream they discovered the poles where too short to reach bottom. Thus they were left to the mercy of the tide which swept them back out and there they fell easy victim to the Union troops. General Trapier also reported why so few men were left to guard Cedar Key, the Gulf terminal of the important railroad link across the state. It turns out he was complying with orders to concentrate his forces at Fernandina, thus he had moved the two companies assigned to Cedar Key over to Amelia Island.

It was only after citizens of Cedar Key notified him that they feared that certain persons who had previously been arrested as traitors but later released for lack of evidence, prompted by revenge had reported the lack of Confederate troops to the Union forces, that General Trapier had sent a small force back to protect the populace. Throughout the war, Union forces were repeatedly tipped-off by sympathizers and traitors. Additionally large gangs of men who refused to serve either in Confederate forces or in the Militia ravaged Florida. Levy County was a hotbed of such activity and considerable Confederate military was wasted trying to control these gangs instead of fighting the war.

On 21 January 1862, the Confederate schooner *Olive Branch*, bound from Cedar Key to Nassau with a cargo of turpentine was captured by the *USS Ethan Allen*. This would be the last Confederate vessel to sail from Cedar Key. Some blockade running by Confederate vessels occurred from Crystal River. The Suwannee was heavily patrolled which limited its use. The Withlacoochee saw no action as the mouth was too shallow to allow Confederate vessels to get upriver and away from Federal gunboats. The Wacasassa, however, would see much action.

On 24 May 1862, John C. Chambers, at his own expense got up a company of some 80 enlisted men and 5 officers called the Gulf Coast Rangers. Later they would be incorporated into the Confederate Army as Company A Florida 9th Infantry. Reports indicate these men originally met at Station No. 4 on the Florida Railroad and it would be back at this location that the only significant battle of the war in Levy County would take place. Confederate troops were constantly monitoring Yankee fortifications and activities at Cedar Keys from this position and they observed troops massing for operations inland in February of 1865. Word was sent and Capt. J. J. Dickinson was ordered to engage the enemy as their movement and control of the area to the north would cut the important road between Tallahassee and West Florida from East Florida. The Yankees after capturing horses, cattle, cotton and other materials, and meeting some limited resistance began to fall back to their base at Cedar Keys.

Feeling safe and needing rest, they camped at Station 4 on the evening of February 12, 1865. About 7 A.M. on the morning of February 13, 1865, Yankee pickets fired on the advancing Confederate forces under Capt. John J. Dickinson which consisted of 90 cavalry troops, 52 from Company H, Second Florida Cavalry commanded by Lt's McCardell and McEaddy; Company B of the same regiment, with 18 men commanded by Lt's McLeod and Stephens (author's Great Grandfather); Company H 5th Battalion, commanded by Lt's Haynes, Brantley and Haile with 20 men; also Capt. Lutterloh of the local militia with 18 men commanded by Captain King, Dudley, Prince and Waterson. The total force being some 145 men but only 120 were engaged as the remainder was with the horses and one piece of artillery.

The Yankees were forced to abandon many of their dead and most of the plunder they had taken from local Confederate sympathizers. Capt. Dickinson drove the Yankees back to Cedar Keys and reported the entire force would have been slaughtered had it not been for his Confederate forces running out of ammunition. Yankee troops under Major Weeks numbered 386 from the Second Regiment of U. S. Colored Troops and Second Regiment Florida Cavalry.

An artist rendition of the events of the Battle of Fort # 4. Courtesy of Florida State Archives Photo Collection.

On 31 August 1862 they reported to Fort Brooke (Tampa) under orders of Brigadier General Joseph Finegan, commander of Florida forces. Captain Chamber's Company A, along with five other companies, joined for review and inspection by General Finegan. The General then issued orders for deployment to various locations around the state. Captain Chambers was assigned to Bayport near the mouth of the Weekiwachee River, arriving 10 October 1862. He then directed two detachments to posts along the coast. One Sergeant, a Corporal and 13 privates under Lt. Hogans went to Homosassa and another of the same composition under Lt. Lane to Crystal River.

Capt. Chambers remained with the main body of his Company at Bayport until 10 October 1863 when he was allowed to resign for bad health. Due to the extreme need for manpower, men were not allowed to resign in such a manner unless seriously sick and most often even then were required to join the local militia when they returned to their homes, thus Chambers must have indeed been quite ill, and perhaps not expected to recover.

Following Chambers' resignation, Lt. E. A. Davis was promoted to Captain. A few months later the company was ordered north and would see action at the Battle of Olustee near Lake City. From there they would be ordered to

Virginia, joining General Lee's troops and fighting at Petersburg, Va., Bull Run, and Cold Harbor.

One of the Levy County soldiers in this company was Oliver Hazard Perry Kirkland. Sergeant Kirkland sought and received a 30 day furlough in February 1865 while the two opposing armies were in winter quarters in Virginia. When the time came to return north from Levy County, Union Troops had control of all crossings on the Savannah River and it seemed likely he would be unable to return to his company. Accordingly, O. H. P. Kirkland was encouraged to attach himself to some local Confederate command so as to not be deemed a deserter. Capt. Lutterloh, in command of the local militia, was in need of a Pilot on the Wekiva and Wacasassa Rivers at Gulf Hammock and Kirkland volunteered to fill the position.

It was here that word eventually reached them that the war was ended and they should report to Union forces at Cedar Key. Under flag of truce, Capt. Lutterloh, Dr. J. M. Jackson and Sgt. Kirkland reported to Yankee Lt. Stubbins at Cedar Key. Lt. Stubbins ordered them to muster all Confederate forces at the Bronson Courthouse where they were given the oath and paroled.

John C. Chambers is not found in the 1870 census and from deed research, it appeared he might have died as early as 1865; however the author found him in the 1880 census living at Orange Lake in Marion County. He no longer is living alone but is found in the household of his brother, B. R. Chambers. Perhaps he had been here since resigning from the war and they have nursed him back to health. Also in the area are several other families from South Carolina. By 1880 the sawmill had certainly been long closed and forgotten as in January of that year, George Moody purchased Chambers Island from the State of Florida (see Florida DEP doc. 203122).

Several Chambers relatives followed him to Florida from South Carolina including Mrs. Elizabeth S. Chambers, his widowed mother, and brothers William Ellison Chambers and Samuel C. Chambers. James S. Chambers lived at Black Dirt in 1860. In 1870 Mary Chambers lived in Cedar Key and W.E. Chambers lived near Andrew E. Hodges' Magnolia Plantation and they were close friends.

Dr. Andrew Elton Hodges

The next important pioneer of Levy County was Dr. Andrew Elton Hodges. Much as been previously written about him and much of that is not supported by the evidence. Several stories about him have made their way into newspapers over the years and while they are lovely, fanciful stories, and may even help to sell newspapers, they are not factual. After I had accumulated considerable research materials on Dr. Hodges and began comparing the various stories, it became clear that much of what had been written probably came from one early source. Texas Ruffus Hodges, son of Dr. Hodges, is attributed as the author of an early history of this pioneer and his family. There exists several typed histories attributed to him, each differing somewhat. One has to wonder whether the various typists made changes or T.R. himself made changes over time. He was called T. R. as an adult but Ruff (pronounced roof) as a child and he was the tenth born. In 1885, when his father died, he was just 10 years of age so it is questionable whether he would have accumulated his supposed wealth of family history stories directly from Dr. Hodges. His mother lived until 1911, so he undoubtedly acquired some stories of the family from her.

Dr. Hodges is said to have desired one of his four young sons to act as his constant companion, to accompany him at all times on his many rounds of business. He selected the youngest of the four, Ruff, the day before his sixth birthday and decided to give him a test as a horseman. He told Ruff to climb on one of his best horses and ride him. The horse balked and dumped Ruff on the ground but he got up and climbed back and rode off. The Doctor was satisfied that Ruff could do the job. They rode on separate horses, slept and

31

ate together, and once a week they would return home for a one day visit and change of clothes. His father was a good teacher and taught him until he attended school with the rest of the children. Ruff would remain the constant companion until he was nine. It is quite possible that the stories T.R. would later tell were "yarns" told around the campfire by his father during this period, and the young boy would naturally take them literally.

Truth! What is the truth? Most people when telling their family's history don't tell the whole story. For one thing, they can only tell of their experience, stories that older relatives chose to share with them and whatever facts they have discovered in research. Stories also generally change over time. They may become embellished or "toned down". Experiences not believed "worthy" of remembering aren't, just as failures are often conveniently forgotten. So it is left to impartial researchers to search out the facts. With the clear view of 20-20 hindsight, we can see important factors in the development of a family that may not have been realized at the time. The author doesn't claim his research on this family is conclusive but sufficient proof has been identified that we can be sure of many changes needed to correct the previous "histories".

The various editions of T.R. Hodges' story usually begin with a wonderful love story. The good Doctor, for whatever reason, decides to sell most of his property in Dooley County, Georgia and migrate to the new territory of Florida. As T.R. tells it, *"Reserving six of his best slaves, 12 of his best horses, six blooded cows and a bull....four covered wagons, a carriage and buggy, together with household furniture and farming tools...."* Arriving at the Georgia-Florida border, he leaves all his wealth in the care of his overseer. The story tells us that his boyhood sweetheart had migrated earlier with her family to Texas from her home in Georgia or Alabama. The years 1844 and 1854 are often given for when this occurred. The 1844 an obvious error since the Doctor would only have been some 14 years of age. "After a brief courtship......." they returned to Florida. A trip to Texas from Georgia in 1854 was anything but brief....and courtships, even of previous childhood sweethearts were not "brief". The truth, according to the Doctor's widow, is that they didn't marry until 1856. Complicating the issue further, she states that she was born not in Georgia or Alabama, but in Montgomery County,

Texas. (The proof being Florida Confederate Widow's Pension Application D12551); and he couldn't have kept "six of his best slaves" because he never had that many!

From the 1850 U.S. Census we can confirm the Hodges family in Dooley County, Georgia, 24th District, household #203, consisting of: (John) Elbert Hodges, 47, a mechanic; Silence (Culpepper), 37; Andrew E., 20, a farmer; Joel C., 16; Benjamin 11; Mary Ann, 9; William E., 4; and Robert 1, all born in Georgia. In 1850, primogeniture was still the practice (i.e. the oldest son would inherit all the land). Older brother Edmond K. Hodges, is living with his family in Randolph, Ga. Sister Julia also is not with the family so we can presume she was by this time married and in her own household at this census. So with primogeniture the practice and indeed the law of the land, younger sons, like Andrew, were destined to seek their fortunes elsewhere thus was further encouraged the migration into new territory in search of land.

Sometime after 1850 and prior to going off to Texas, Andrew Hodges allegedly attended Medical School. It is reported that he went to school in Charleston, South Carolina, and we know the Medical School of South Carolina at Charleston was in operation at that time, but a review of records proves Hodges never attended! At that time in our country's history it was not required to have college training prior to attending medical school. Formal medical training usually consisted of only one year although some studied for two, but many men simply apprenticed with a physician and learned to be a Doctor by "on-the-job" training, and at some point, when most of their patients survived, they were deemed qualified to practice medicine on their own. The Medical School of Georgia was also in operation in the 1850s, but as yet we have been unable to determine if he attended school at that institution either as this manuscript goes to press. Probably Hodges simply acquired his medical training by apprenticeship, perhaps in Charleston, thus leading to the story of his attending medical school there.

While we know with certainty the young Doctor didn't pursue a "childhood sweetheart" to Texas, we will probably never be sure what the real purpose of the trip was. Perhaps he simply followed others that he had known back in Dooley County, Georgia, typical of the time. A search of the 1850 Georgia Census proves his Georgia neighbors, the Outlaws, Olivers, and Hawkins families had left the same area of Georgia for Texas about the same time as Hodges. John C. Sheffield, close neighbor and friend in Georgia would later help bail him out of jail in Texas so perhaps Hodges actually went to Texas to visit this good friend. We can be certain that by the fall of 1855 he was in Guadalupe County near the town Seguin (just east of San Antonio), for it was here that his temper (he had red hair and a temper to go with it) would get him into trouble, something that he would experience again in Levy County.

Dr. Andrew Elton Hodges had red hair and beard and is said to "have a temper to go with it".
Photo courtesy of Hodges descendant, Ray Mason.

On 25 December 1855, probably at a holiday "frolic" he got into a fight with John Christopher. Perhaps John asked Nancy Johnson to dance or perhaps "made eyes at her", but whatever the reason, Hodges "called him out" and got into a fight. A short time later the Sheriff arrested Hodges for "assault with intent to kill"! Being far from home and without finances, Hodges sought help from Nancy's family. On 3 January 1856 the bond was set at $2,500 and was posted by Nancy's brother W.H.C. Johnson, three of her brothers-in-law, Miles Elkins, A.E. Knowles and Joseph Hawkins, with help from other friends and possibly family relations, John C. Sheffield, P.R. Oliver and Y. P. (Pinkney) Outlaw. Hodges was ordered to not leave the county but to await trial at the next Term of the District Court in the spring.

Nancy Pinkney Maldonata Johnson, photo courtesy of Hodges descendant, Ray Mason.

Not wanting to wait for the trial, Hodges married Nancy Pinkney Maldonata Johnson on 6 January 1856, and immediately escaped Texas by running off to Florida! (Author's note: While you may think it curious that a criminal in Texas in the mid 1800s would seek escape from the law by running off to Florida, this was not unusual at all! Florida was much more the Frontier at that time than was Texas, and many people "escaped" to Florida. This author is aware of two such men who ended up here in south Levy County!)

At the spring court term, Hodges of course failed to appear as ordered nor did his bondsmen, therefore the court found him guilty and the bond forfeited. Curiously the bondsmen would appeal the ruling on various technical grounds. The case would eventually reach the Texas Supreme Court in 1857, but of course they would lose the case and their money (see Appendix A). Incredibly they would appeal again on a clerical error and this would reach the Texas Supreme Court in 1860 (see Appendix B) where they would again lose.

Arriving in Florida they passed through Gator (near present day Lake City) and Worthington Springs in Alachua County, before arriving in Ocala where T.R.'s story indicates there were "a few scattered houses...a pine mill and cotton gin". Ocala, even in 1856, which would have been about when the Doctor and his new bride actually arrived in Florida, was anything but a "village". Ocala had originally been established about ten years earlier, an outgrowth from old Fort King located just to the east. There was a fine city square, numerous businesses and a jail. Surrounding the square were numerous residences and around town were considerable farmers. Doctor Hodges, after scouting the surrounding area, is said to have settled in southwest Marion County. One story alleges he bought the springs west of Dunnellon that would later be owned by Albertus Vogt and where he would allegedly discover phosphate but this author has found no deeds to prove these stories.

In the 1860 Florida Census we find the Doctor, age 30, not in Marion County but living in Levy County in Black Dirt District (ie. Southern Levy County) in household #180 with his wife Nancy P. M. age 20. His occupation is listed as physician-farmer and his real property valued at $1,600 and personal property at $1,025. Note that he is a "farmer", not planter, the difference being that a planter would have 10 or more slaves to work the cotton and other field crops. Thus whatever wealth was to be his in the future would come from his hands, not from a wealthy aristocratic family. Later claims that many slaves were used to construct his plantation homes and cut lime rock for wharfs are also difficult to reconcile with the fact that he had few slaves and none were male!

Living with him in 1860 were two younger brothers, William E. age 16, Robert T. age 11, and his own two children born since arriving in Florida, Antonio De Lopez (called Leo) age 3 and Romulus Robert age 1. The Doctor possesses only two slaves, 9 and 40 year old females. Living nearby is his brother Joel Culpepper Hodges age 25, a farmer and his wife Mahala age 22 and their son Glen Tyler age 1, and no slaves.

The older Hodges boys: Ruff, Randolph, Jules, Yulee and Culpepper ca. 1936. Photo courtesy of Hodges descendant Ray Mason.

Black Dirt

The first white community in southern Levy County was Black Dirt. It was a farming community which grew up from what had been Fort Clinch. Built during the Second Seminole War in October 1836, the fort was located on the road leading from Clay Landing on the Suwannee River. The road crossed the Withlacoochee River at Fort Clinch thence on south to Fort Brooke (Tampa). (See *Map of Wacassassa River accompanying report of Capt E. Backus of a scout of said river and Gulf of Mexico, 1839,* National Archives RG 77, L 247-51). The fort was abandoned in May 1842. It was again briefly occupied by Confederate troops but by that time was of no military importance and these troops were soon called away.

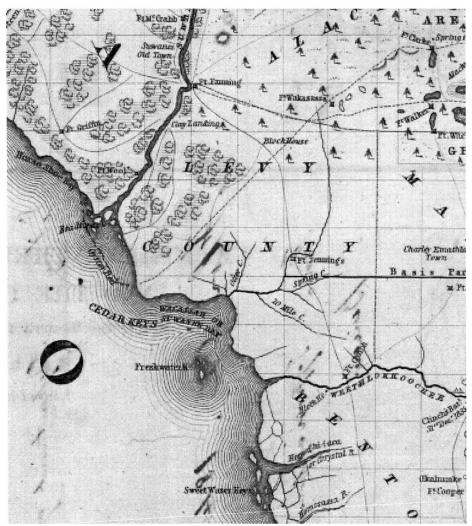

Map depicting the area which would later become Levy County. From the Library of Congress Digital Map Collection, showing Ft. Clinch on the Withlacoochee Road.

Black Dirt community continued to grow and a Post Office was established 5 July 1856 with Joseph A. Everett as Postmaster. A.E. Hodges replaced him as Postmaster 6 October 1859. With the establishment of other communities following the Civil War, Black Dirt waned. Eventually the Post Office was disestablished on 29 March 1867. Southern Levy County would continue to be known as the Black Dirt District or simply as Black Dirt for many years.

As late as March 1861 there were only two houses in Crystal River. Goods were brought by boat from Cedar Key. Salted fish and goods were then shipped by wagon to Ocala. The road went north to Hodges Ferry (the first of two ferries the Doctor would operate) at Black Dirt then on past Juliet to Ocala. No doubt when the military occupied Fort Clinch they operated a ferry. When Dr. Hodges decided to settle in the area family oral history relates that he operated a ferry in this location. The oldest Levy County Board of County Commissioners Minutes Book is missing thus the only proof of the ferry is from several old maps (See: (1) 1859 Surveyor General Map, Library of Congress, which was created to accompany the annual report. It is a township map showing drainage, cities and towns, railroads, location of the land grant railroads. It shows the military road from Clay Landing to Fort Clinch and river crossing. (2) 1865 General Topographical Map Sheet XI, Atlas to Accompany the Official Records of the Union and Confederate Armies, Library of Congress courtesy of private collector Roy Winkelman. It shows the various roads thru Levy County. Fort Clinch is now identified as Black Dirt where the road continues across the river. This would be Hodges first ferry).

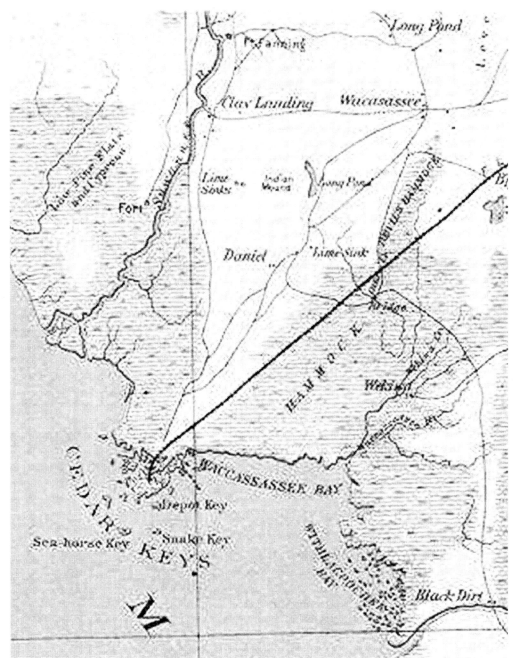

Map now shows the Withlacoochee River crossing point as Black Dirt.

Typical ferry of the period courtesy of Florida State Archives Photo Collection.

In April 1862, Dr. Hodges formed a company of Home Guard to patrol the coast. He was the Captain, his brother Joel was the First Lieutenant and the Second Lieutenant was William Bertine. The company was composed of 75-80 men and boys, some as young as 12. The Company was divided into three squads. One stationed at Bear Landing on the lower Withlacoochee, one was at the Rocks on the Crystal River and the other on an island near the mouth of the Homosassa River. Despite its small size, the Homosassa River was deemed the most likely to be attacked by the Union forces due to the David Yulee's sugar mill and plantation. Sugar and syrup were processed at the mill and what was not used locally was shipped to Cedar Key by boat and thence by railroad to Fernandina and other markets.

David Yulee's Florida Railroad had completed the railroad link between Fernandina and Cedar Keys 15 March 1861, when the engine Abner McGehee pulled into Cedar Key Station. The Abner McGehee (sometimes miss-spelled McGahee) had originally been built for sawmill operator Abner McGehee, owner of the Montgomery Railroad on 26 April 1839. It was a

Rogers Company engine (construction no. 12) and had been purchased for construction of the Florida Railroad but due to the onset of war and shortage of engines, it was continued in operation hauling people and goods.

Photo courtesy of Florida State Archives photo collection.

At the time Florida became a state in 1845, there was only one railroad in operation and it with only 23 miles of track connecting Tallahassee with **St. Marks**. Farmers relied entirely on water transportation and desperately desired a railroad connection with the center of the state and thence to the ports of Savannah and Charleston. The stakes in the development of railroad was high. David Yulee had promoted statehood with the proposal that the state build a railroad from the Gulf to the Atlantic using the 500,000 acres of land the state was to receive from the Federal Government. He even suggested this proposed state-owned railroad would pay all the costs of the state government! Projects were slow to get under way as capitol was beyond the resources of the promoters.

In 1853 the Florida General Assembly had chartered the Florida Railroad Company to build a line from some port on the Atlantic to some port on the Gulf Coast, now all they needed was funding. In 1851 the General Assembly had created the Internal Improvement Board to manage the swamp and "overflowed" lands and the 500,000 acres of public land transferred from the Federal Government. By 1854 the Board had determined the priority should be for a system of railroads to connect Jacksonville, Fernandina,

Pensacola, and Tampa and also for a Canal connecting the St. Johns River with the Indian River down the east coast of the state.

The General Assembly in 1855 created the Internal Improvement Fund, composed of the Governor and 4 other senior state officials. Railroad and canal projects which received their approval could receive assistance in the manner of 200 feet of right-of-way through any state owned lands and alternate sections of land, 6 miles deep on both sides. Furthermore, when the railroad grade had been constructed and crossties laid, the railroads could issue bonds up to $10,000 per mile for the purchase of rolling stock and rails.

Work finally began on the Florida Railroad in 1855 as they had decided the most advantageous route would be from Fernandina to Cedar Keys. Yulee and his supporters had chosen not only to build a line to serve residents and businesses along the route but also to move passengers and freight from sea-going vessels at either terminal across the state to avoid the long sea journey around the peninsula. Yulee had hoped the railroad could be owned by Floridians, even allowing the purchase of stock with only ten percent down payment. Eventually they would have to seek other financing and sold a controlling interest in the line to E. M. Dickerson and Associates of Boston which allowed them to complete the project.

Cedar Keys wharf area. Photo from the Cedar Key Historical Society.

Although the completion of the line marked a new era in Florida by opening up a vast area for development and by furnishing the long awaited coast to coast route, there were many who opposed the railroad. Crackers claimed the turpentine operations which were developed as a result of the railroad ruined their hog ranges and that the engines killed their cattle; farm wives reported their eggs being broken when trying to cross the tracks with their carts.

The railroads thus developed were largely designed to access the interior of the state rather than make connections to other states. In fact, in 1860 with the advent of the Civil War, the only railroad connection northward was west of the Chattahoochee River over the Florida and Alabama Railroad which connected Pensacola to Alabama. The lack of overland transportation capabilities would prove disastrous in the coming war.

On 19 April 1861, President Lincoln issued his Proclamation of Blockade Against Southern Ports which would bring disaster to Cedar Key as it attracted Union Troops. In a few months the federal blockade was set up along Florida's coast and Federal Troops would occupy Cedar Key on 16 January 1862. Florida's lengthy coastline proved difficult to blockade and the state would soon become the "breadbasket" of the Confederacy. Most blockades running along the Levy County coast would be from the Wacasassa River with large quantities of cotton and some naval stores (turpentine) were being shipped from the area along with salt and fish. The Withlacoochee River with the extremely shallow waters at the mouth on both sides of Chambers Island was too treacherous and the mouth of the Suwannee was too heavily guarded by blockading vessels out of Cedar Key.

Following the Civil War, Hodges began purchasing cedar lands along the Withlacoochee in both Levy and Citrus Counties and in the Gulf Hammock. Over the next ten years he would accumulate several thousand acres. Cedar logs would be felled by axe and dragged out by teams of oxen to property the Doctor owned on the river at a place that would come to be called Cedar Landing (located at the end of present day Elkins Street in Inglis). Here they would be rafted together and towed to the mills at Cedar Key. One such towboat was the Yulee, Captained by Sam Reddick.

Eight pair of oxen hitched to a "high wheeler" for dragging the heavy logs from swamp or boggy land. The front of the log would be carried by the narrow axle between the high wheels preventing it from digging into the ground thus allowing the log to be slid along. Photo courtesy of Florida State Archives Photo Collection.

In 1866 Hodges purchased two parcels of land in present day Yankeetown that he would develop as farms, one was called Cherry Hammock and it would be here that he would move the family sometime between 1867 and 1870 and the farm at Black Dirt would be sold in 1872. Soon a small community would develop that would become known as Hodges (the first of two such places in this area).

Other writers have speculated Doctor Hodges settled on Hickory Island following the Civil War, building a "summer" home and starting a farming operation. Until recently we were only able to confirm Hodges had been deeded the property as a homestead in 1880, proving only that he would have "improved" the property for at least the previous five years. Then, quite by accident, the author discovered a business arrangement with Simeon Jones. In June of 1866, Jones died. In his probate file we find that he was "a member of the firm Andrew Hodges And Company". They were in the cedar business and had made an arrangement to harvest considerable acreage. In a petition to the Judge of Probate, the widow Civility Jones, states that following harvest of a large number of cedar logs (in the Gulf Hammock just north of present day Inglis) at considerable expense, the value of cedar had dropped to the extent that the sale of the logs would not cover the costs of the logging operation, thus the estate was greatly in debt. Doctor Hodges suggested she give him some 960 acres of property, including their home, and he would assume the debt on the cedar harvest. Thus on 17 December 1866 we find a deed made out to Hodges by Civility Jones (see Levy Co Deed Book A, page 23) selling him the 960 acres for $1.00. What does this have to do with Hickory Island you ask? In the probate file is a curious document. It seems that in November 1866 Col. W. R. Coulter, attorney for the widow Jones, met with Doctor Hodges to discuss settlement of the debt and wrote out a description of the lands to be included in the proposed deed. In accordance with custom of the day, the top margin of that document includes the date and location where the document was prepared, "Hodges Island, 7 Nov. 1866". So from this we can be certain that Hodges was indeed on the island late in 1866 although he would not apply for a government deed for some fifteen years.

Hickory Island home ca. 1906. Child to left is Cullie Durand, on right is Rand (William Randolph Hodges, Sr.)

We can only speculate as to how much of a "friend" or business partner Hodges was to Jones when he acquired the widow's home and all that land for just $1.00 and her release from the supposed logging debt. Hodges continued to harvest cedar logs and amazingly there is no further report of excessive costs involved with that harvest, leaving us to wonder if the "suspicious" sudden debt appeared only due to Jones' untimely death.

Charles B. "Charlie" Rogers

A young man by the name of Charles B. Rogers was in Jacksonville in route to Cedar Key to visit his uncle, E. J. Lutterloh, a lawyer, but he was without a cent of money and the only way he could get to Cedar Key was by the railroad. He applied to the agent who told him he would have to buy a ticket but with no money, what was he to do? He was allowed to make the trip by acting as car duster and cleaner. Upon arrival in Cedar Key, the uncle advised him to get into some kind of business and probably advanced some money.

Edward J. Lutterloh. Photo courtesy of Florida State Archives photo collection.

In the 1870 census we find C. B. Rogers living with Lutterloh and working as a railroad clerk. Rogers is said to also have opened a little shop on the head of the railroad dock, selling peanuts, crackers and other light foods. Doctor Hodges made weekly trips to Cedar Key in his schooner and tied up at the dock where Charlie had his little shop. Hodges was sympathetic and wanted to help Charlie out and told him to send all his stock down to the boat and paid him full retail prices. This was repeated weekly until Charlie had accumulated considerable money and opened up a shop in town under the name of Charles B. Rogers & Company in 1879.

C.B. Rogers & Co. store after the 1896 storm. Photo courtesy Florida State Archives Photo Collection.

Charlie was always on the lookout for some advantage and soon found someone to invest in his business.

Mr. Wolfe from a community named North in South Carolina (located on the Westside of Orangeburg County, south of Columbia, S.C.), was a wealthy land owner with a large cotton operation. His two sons, Fred and Pete, had heard of Cedar Key and thought it might be a good place to locate a business. Fred was married, but Pete was single. Mr. Wolfe brought them down by train and after looking over the area, he set Fred up in a nice store on the north side of D and 2nd Streets. They hired local Dick Hodgson as clerk and Fred built his home down D Street across from 6th street.

Charles Rogers was on the lookout for a prosperous person like Mr. Wolfe and engaged him in the prospect of joining Rogers in business. Charlie proposed a partnership with Pete, and thinking this a good idea, Mr. Wolfe thus invested several thousand dollars. Meantime Pete started clearing a lot on the south side of D Street, across from 4th Street, so he could build a home. While cleaning out the brush and briars, he stuck a thorn in his arm,

49

developed blood poisoning and within days he was dead. After the funeral, Charlie Rogers denied that Mr. Wolfe had ever paid him any money for a partnership and that he alone owned the building and business. Later he would take another partner, Mr. E. A. Champlain. It is not clear how much Champlain paid if anything, but Champlain and his family moved onto Pete's lot and claimed he owned it! We would expect Doctor Hodges to have known of Rogers cheating the Wolfes, perhaps he didn't think it could happen to him since he had befriended Rogers, but the Hodges family would regret their father's association with Charlie Rogers!

About this time, Andrew E. Hodges would have another bout with the law! In the criminal record books of Levy County in 1867 we find a curious entry indicating Hodges has been charged with murder, and then, quite improperly, the entire entry is marked out and in the margin is written, "error". At the next term of the court in the spring of 1868 he would not be so lucky and the charge of murder would be held to him.

We are indebted to a Johnson family researcher (family of Mrs. Nancy P.M. [Johnson] Hodges) for the following letter written by Narcissa Johnson Hawkins to her sister Matilda Margaret Johnson:

7 December 1867

My Sister Malda Dear:

Your letter came safely hear (sic).
Nothing could have pleased me better
that to received from you a letter.

As I took it to read it I sat down.
The children all gathered round
listening with attentive ear
to hear from their cousins dear.

You say Ma will not come
till after Christmas home
(Ma was their mother, Elizabeth Finley (Cowan) Johnson)
And to be shocked I had no need
At Andrews (Doctor Hodges) dreadful deed.

As he has done the same before
Poor Nan (Mrs. Nancy Hodges) her heart is grieved sore.
Ma will not leave her in grief
until she gains some relief.
(Mother Johnson had come to Florida to be with daughter Nancy).

But relief I fear she cannot find
even a Mother so affectionate and kind
as long as she is Andrew Hodges wife
she cannot lead a pleasant life.

I'm sorry but that does no good
I fain would help her if I could
yet she has a high mind
She would not thank me for words so kind.

In such matters as this
think my words quite amiss
and I hope you'll not let her know
that I expressed myself to you so.

You wrote for me to write to you
About Bettie and Sole, that I'll do (Sole is writer's child)
Bettie says she will write without delay
But she is gone from home today.

Sole is just as fat as he can be
And no trouble at all to me
I go where ever I please
I find myself much at ease.

He is fond of Betty & will stay
At home & not cry when I'm away
I'll move to Sandies before long
Hawk is gone to build a house rough and strong. (writer's husband was Joseph Hawkins)

In which you'll find us when you come
We will welcome you to our rude home
With joyful hearts we'll all greet you
Your husband & your children too.

I'm sorry it never entered into my head
To write you Bro. Miles wife was dead (Miles is writer's brother-in-law, Miles Hawkins)
And while she from Earth's cares are freed
Left in much trouble indeed.

While his heart within him is in pain
At the thought that he will never see her again
From that you know he can't refrain
Though his loss is her eternal gain.

Two wives to the bright realms of glory gone
An left poor Miles hear (sic) on earth alone
Though I expect this poor Brother
Will get himself another.

You right (sic) that Bam will go
With her Uncle John to Waco
Where she will see
A beautiful Christmas tree

Bettie and myself does not expect to be
In any gay place or company
But I expect to try if I can
*To be in the society of sister **Ann**.*

And I do believe Sister that you
Had rather be in our company too
On next Christmas day
Than to assemble with the gay.

Well as it is almost night
And have nothing much to write
Perhaps you'll think I'd better
Conclude this simple letter.

Miles, Auty, Billy and Bettie too
All send there (sic) love to you
But one thing more I must say
I went to church the other day

And herd (sic) Hezy exhort and pray (Hezekiah Williams, writer's nephew)
And sing a joyful Christian lay
I had the pleasure of offering my hand
To one of my kindred in the stand

Dear Malda I often pray
For you who is so far away
Although I write this in rime (sic)
That god may save you in this trying time.
Tell Bill I've heaved many sighs

About his poor sore eyes
Do tell him to come out hear (sic)
And see his old sister dear.

One word to me you did not tell
About Mary and Telephus whether sick or well (writer's brother Telephus
Johnson and his wife Mary Ann Winslow)
Write on what part of the ground
Mary and Tell may be found.

Do tell John and his pretty wife Tee (writer's brother John Dillard Johnson
and his wife Matilda Margaret Johnson)
To come out to see Hawk and me
You are tired of this I do suppose
Next time I'll write in prose

The last that I will tell
All the conexcion (sic) is well
One thing more I'll say to you
Write soon & often too.

Tell Mr. Lackland to be sure to try (Sam Lackland, husband of Malda, to
whom the letter is addressed)
And bring you all in July
So I bid you all good by

Now my name to this I'll fix
You'll find it is your sister Nix.

Andrew Hodges was indicted for the murder of Benjamin Leak and surprisingly demanded an immediate trial which was granted. As yet we have not been unable to locate the file at the Levy County Clerk's Office on this case to learn the particulars so all we know is that Doctor Hodges again slipped through the hands of justice and in this case he was acquitted (indications being that the demand and approval of a speedy trial didn't allow for the necessary witnesses to arrive for the trial).

In the summer of 1870, Nancy Hodges was expecting her eighth child. William Randolph Hodges (called Rand) would be born in July. Customary to that time, little Leona Hodges, age 4, was sent down the road to live with friends, W. E. Chambers and his family where she could play with her buddy William, age 6 where she is found living when the Federal Census of 1870 was recorded in June.

In 1879 Dr. Hodges purchased property just north of Inglis along present day Butler Road that he would call Magnolia Plantation; Bought from the daughter of a friend, General Jesse Carter, her name was Josephine (called Josie) and this pretty young thing would do what many other young lovelies have done to older married men, namely their beauty would cause excitement, joy and T R O U B L E !

Various family stories indicate that the Doctor intended to hire a tutor for the younger children, common practice at the time. Wife Nancy allegedly tells her husband not to bring home a "comely looking young woman". When Josie arrives, wife Nancy allegedly departs with the youngest children for Cedar Key. We can be certain the Doctor knew Josie as early as the land sale in 1879 and it appears that by 1882 Josie is living with the Hodges family because the Doctor paid her with an IOU in amount $100 "for service rendered". Josie would continue to live and "work" for Hodges until his death in 1885. Wife Nancy finally had enough of this arrangement and left for Cedar Key with daughter May some time early in 1884. Adding to this confusion is a family story that the Doctor hired a Mr. Warren to teach the older boys and Eva Reeford to teach the small children, but neither of these names is found in any census or other record with the Hodges family or anywhere else in Levy County during this period of time.

Cedar was very valuable and many fights and arguments arose over logging. Much of the land had still not been homesteaded or purchased from the government. Men simply located a good stand of timber and began harvesting, paying no attention to land boundaries. On May 18, 1881, Dr. Hodges was sued in Levy County Circuit Court for harvesting 499 sticks (logs) of cedar off land he didn't own. The case would languish in the courts for years and eventually would reach the Florida Supreme Court in 1896, by this time the assessed damages for the thievery would be $1,362.27 and interest of $1,216.11 and this didn't include the considerable court costs (see Appendix C).

Much has been written and told of the Doctor building a school on Schoolhouse Island (thus giving the island that name) but the only proof is in these oral histories. In 1883 the Doctor attempted to sell this property and listed an advertisement in the newspaper *The Levy Enterprise*:

"HICKORY ISLAND FARM is situated on the Gulf Coast about 20 miles south of Cedar Keys on an island and contains 165 acres of land – 40 acres under cultivation; a grove of five hundred orange trees – 50 of which are now in bearing; and the balance will bear in two years; besides lemons, limes, peaches, plums, guavas, gigs, pecans, &c., all in bearing; and being situated on the Gulf there is an abundance of game, such as deer, turkeys &c. A good residence containing 8 rooms with outhouses, a well of good water and large cistern; and excellent wharf for landing and lading of boats, a good storeroom and office convenient to the wharf. Hickory Island is connected with the main land by a good shell turnpike. Price $6,000. For particulars address Dr. E. O. Paschall at Bronson, or Dr. A. E. Hodges, Cedar Key, Fla."

This acreage included Schoolhouse Island, but the advertisement lists no improvements on that island such as a schoolhouse.

Hodges

As previously stated, the first community by the name of Hodges (there would be two) was established on the north bank of the Withlacoochee River by Andrew E. Hodges on land he owned and farmed in present day

Yankeetown, a farm he called Cherry Hammock, here he would establish his second ferry.

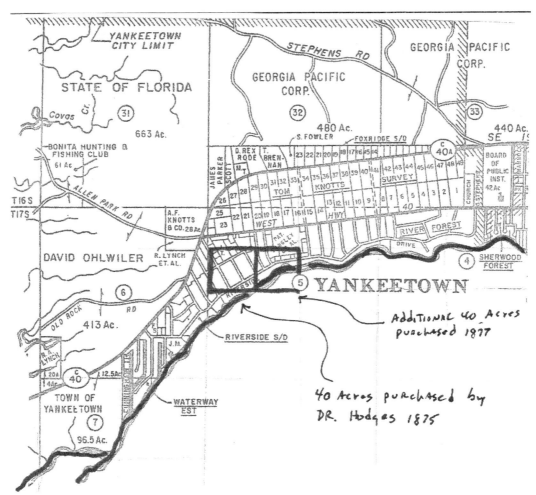

Sidney Lanier, a poet from Macon, Georgia, who had not yet met with great success and needing money for his family, reluctantly agreed to write a guidebook for the Atlantic Coastline Railroad. He also mentioned his support for a cross state water link! He wrote, "There is an inside passage from Cedar Keys to this point (Withlacoochee) and one of the most important projects, it would seem, that has been mooted in Florida, is one to connect the Withlacoochee River with the Ocklawaha by canal, for which a charter has already been obtained by Colonel Hart, of Pilatka (sic). An astonishingly small amount of labor would accomplish this end, and would thus render practicable a clear water-way across the entire peninsula of Florida from the Gulf to the Atlantic. Lake Panasofka, which has the Withlacoochee for its outlet into the Gulf, is but 13 miles from Lake Harris, whose outlet is the Ocklawaha, flowing into the St. Johns, to the Atlantic Ocean."

Kirk Munroe had been a popular writer of short stories and editor of *Harper's Young People*. He was an adventurer and avid boater being at the time Commodore of the New York Canoe Club. His sister married a son of Harriet Beecher Stowe and this relationship brought him an invitation to visit the writer's winter home in Florida near Jacksonville. He resigned his position with Harper's to become a free-lance writer and soon headed south.

He came to Florida bringing with him his sailing canoe *Psyche*. During the winter of 1881-1882, he made a trip from the Okeefenokee Swamp, down the Suwannee River to the Cedar Keys, along the coast to Key West. Excerpts from his diary:

"Tuesday, 13 December 1881. Got off this morning though in teeth of strong East wind against which I have paddled all day making 20 miles. Am spending night on Hickory Island in storehouse owned by Dr. Hodges. House nearby is deserted and there is not a soul on island. Found graveyard in midst of grove of bitter oranges. Navigation today has been very difficult on account of numberless small Keys and reefs of oyster rock. Crossed Wacasassa Bay and am within four miles of mouth of Withlacoochie (sic) River."

"Wednesday, 14 December 1881. Shortly after daylight saw Dr. Hodges' sloop with him on board standing-in towards landing. Then took *Psyche* a mile up creek where Dr. has landing. Team met us there and we drove 5 miles to Dr.'s place on Withlacoochie (sic), stopping at Bonita, another of his places, on the way. Went hunting with negro boys in Gulf Hammock in afternoon. Saw one deer but got nothing. Similar success on Fire Hunt in evening. Got very wet on latter during hard rain which lasted nearly all night. Cold 'norther' is setting in"

"Thursday, 15 December 1881. Cold day with strong 'norther' blowing. Left Hickory Island at noon and made Crystal River, which is marked by shell island on south side of mouth at 3:30 o'clock. Made Willis Island 4 miles up the river shortly after 5 o'clock and am stopping with Willis—regular Cracker family, windows with shutters instead of glass..."

Sometime after his wife left him with daughters Leona and May, Hodges made out a will. It is a curious document for several reasons and is undated. From the ages of the children as mentioned in the document, we deduce it was written in 1884, a year before his death (see Appendix D).

It was proved and accepted by the Court of Probate at his death. Just about everyone that had ever done business with Hodges filed claims and suits against the estate including the widow! In his will Hodges had declared all his assets should pass to his "four sons, Culpepper now about sixteen, Randolph now about fourteen, Jules now about twelve and Ruff now about ten years old". Hodges also named Charles B. Rogers as the executor and *guardian* of the boys. Writing his wife and daughter out of his will, and even naming Rogers guardian of the boys seems to indicate a lot of anger and spite, and of course was not legal as we will see later in the story.

In the 1885 Florida State Census A. E. Hodges, age 54, is listed as a Cedar Merchant living in Cedar Key "District" (i.e. the entire coast of Levy County was the district). We know he was living at the community he called Hodges which was located on the Withlacoochee River (near present day Izaak Walton Lodge) since on 6 April 1885, he applied for a permit to operate a ferry at this location (his second ferry). With him are sons Culpepper, William Randolph (Sr.), Jules and several black laborers. Nancy and daughter May are living in the town of Cedar Key. He was given permission for the ferry, the first on the lower Withlacoochee, and the Board of County Commissioners set the following rates:

Four horse or ox team......75 cents
Two horse or ox team.......50 cents.
Buggy and horse............30 cents
Horse and cart.............30 cents
Man and horse..............25 cents
Footman....................10 cents
Cattle per head............2 cents

"Double the above rates may be charged when service is performed in the night time. The ferry was to be kept open from daylight till dark and no one to be detained longer than 30 minutes, and the ferry to be open at any time for an officer in the discharge of his duties or a person in a case of emergency". (see Levy County Board of County Commission Book B, page 248)

Typical ferry of the period courtesy of Florida State Archives Photo Collection.

Doctor Hodges had pushed the establishment of a Post Office but one was not established until after his death. Henry White was named the Postmaster when it was opened on 30 July 1886. Without the Doctor, the community had not prospered, thus the Post Office was disestablished a few months later on 18 November 1886. Culpepper J. Hodges may have continued to operate the ferry started by his father but soon was informed that he would need to file the appropriate application to operate the ferry himself and so on 6 June 1887, he filed a Bond for $500 and the Levy County Commission allowed him to continue to keep the ferry established two years previously by his father. The same rates and restrictions were approved (see Board of County Commission Book B, page 363-364).

Culpepper Hodges photo courtesy of Hodges descendant Ray Mason.

Despite Culpepper's best efforts, this community of Hodges and the ferry were no more successful than had been the efforts of his father, accordingly he shifted his business and residence to Hickory Island. On 3 November 1894 he was allowed to establish a Post Office on Hickory Island at the community (second one) of Hodges with himself as Postmaster. The Post Office would continue in operation until 27 June 1898.

While staying at his Magnolia Plantation (on Butler Road just north of Inglis), the Doctor took ill. They sent for Doctor Charles E. French in Cedar Key. Doctor French and Aunt Hannah (the old x-slave that had been given to Nancy as a wedding gift in Texas) treated Hodges from 16 November until his death on 12 December 1885. The night Hodges died, Aunt Hannah woke the boys (Culpepper, Randolph, Jules and T.R) and they went in to say goodbye to their father. T. R. tells us his father took him by the hand and said, "Son, I am dying, and you must be a good boy." Then he talked to all the boys, telling them that he was leaving five hundred fifty thousand dollars with his good friend, Charlie Rogers and that would take care of them all for a life time. (Authors Note: Merchants like Rogers often provided banking services such as safe keeping of money in their safes for local citizens. This would not be the only case of a citizen losing money entrusted to a merchant in Cedar Key.) The Doctor would die within the hour of talking to the boys. Wife Nancy and daughters May and Leona were in Texas visiting her brother John Dillard Johnson in Waco and were summoned home. Arriving by the first available train, they made their way to Magnolia. A coffin was requested from the undertaker, Mr. Risley, in Cedar Key. He sent one and Doctor Hodges was buried in the family cemetery on Hickory Island. The family returned home from the burial to find a Notice of Appointment of Appraisers, men that would inspect and make a valuation of all Doctor Hodges' property.

In January 1886 the personal property of Hodges was appraised by friends of Charlie Rogers. The sale of this property was held in June and a mere $1,342.08 was collected! The family even had to bid on their own personal things. Mrs. Hodges spent $48.10 purchasing her mare "Kate", a sofa, safe, and wardrobe bedstead.

William Randolph Hodges, Sr. Photo courtesy of Nancy Hodges Duden.

Randolph spent $47.23 purchasing his bed, dining table, some lamps and pictures, tools and implements and an ox cart. Culpepper spent $103.35 purchasing his bed, a table, a watch, some furniture, an ox wagon, some implements, his mare "Dollie", a Ferry and a float. T. R. refused to have anything to do with the sale or with Rogers.

Mrs. Hodges soon filed a petition with the Judge of Probate demanding her Dower Right of 1/3 which was required of the law. She of course won and appraisers were appointed to set aside from the land what she should receive. Under the law she should have been given ownership of 1/3 of the "property where they resided" and 1/3 of the value of the personal property. Instead, she was given lots 13 and 14 in block 1 in Cedar Key and only a life estate on a part (44 acres) of the Hickory Island 160 acres, including the home.

In July of 1886, Rogers sold 135 cedar logs for $279.70 and was required to pay the 1/3 due to Mrs. Hodges. This $93.23 would be the only payment of record by Rogers to the family despite the court order.

Following the sale of the personal property, Rogers and his friend E. A. Champlain packed up and moved to Jacksonville leaving no record of the money Hodges had deposited in Roger's store, nor paying the several debts of the estate.

Rogers would continue to operate the various business enterprises of Doctor Hodges, taking in considerable money and paying out much in expenses to his various friends and business associates. Amazingly, by 1888 the estate was declared insolvent and Rogers was replaced as executor by W. H. Anderson. By this time it was necessary to sell off the other land to pay estate debts. In this, Anderson would prove no more satisfactory than had Rogers.

In order to purchase land for himself, Anderson even had a "Special Master" named to oversee some of the sales. As an example, in 1893 the following acreages were sold for between 10 cents and 35 cents an acre!

Purchaser	Acres	$
A. E. Willard	1,280	160.80
E. W. Agnew	960	130.00
W.H. Anderson	120	13.20

By 1890 there were numerous claims filed against the estate, even Charles Rogers filed another claim! By 1895 it was necessary to even sell the Hickory Island homestead. With a life estate to the widow, there were few willing to even bid, fortunately, Mrs. Hodges was able to buy the islands herself.

Meanwhile Josephine Carter, who had also sued Hodges' estate, had decided to get on with her life and marry Samuel P. Helveston in 1888. She had known him from his cedar business dealings with Doctor Hodges.

Yulee, Randolph, Jules and T.R. received their education at the East Florida Seminary in Gainesville (originally in Ocala, precursor to the University of Florida). The x-slave Hannah, her husband Carey Jackson and their three daughters continued to live and work for the Hodges family for many years in Cedar Key.

Their family wealth stripped from them, the Hodges went to work for various businesses and never heard from Rogers again. Surely they held a grudge as any one would, but there was nothing they could do about the sad situation.

Several years later the old Negro pilot from Cedar Key, Dan McQueen, was in Jacksonville and visited Rogers' Store. McQueen, well familiar with the circumstances asked to see Rogers. A clerk pointed out an old man in a rocking chair but told McQueen not to bother to speak to him as he was "nutty" (Alzheimer's?). The clerk said he had lost his mind so perhaps Rogers got his due.

Pilot Captain Dan W. McQueen. Photo courtesy of Florida State Archives photo collection.

Dan McQueen was a mulatto born into slavery in 1861 Alabama. Following the Civil War he had migrated to Florida and the Suwannee River. In the 1900 census we find him living in Branford with his wife Mollie and son James. His occupation by this time was Captain of a Steamboat on the river. By 1910 he was a Pilot in Cedar Key.

In 1909, when the State of Florida established a Confederate Widow's Pension Fund, Mrs. Hodges was encouraged to apply. Citing Doctor Hodges' organization of the Home Guard Company, she requested the $10.00 per month pension. Unfortunately she may not have been aware that Hodges and the company had been ordered to Confederate service in 1862 and he had disbanded the company rather than comply (he and the men refused to serve since they might have to leave Florida to fight in the war).

How to Procure Land in Florida

The United States acquired large tracts of new territory in the 18th and 19th centuries as foreign countries and Indian tribes ceded land to the federal government. As soon as the government took title to the new land, it became part of the public domain, and both squatters and land speculators rushed to claim it. Once the ceded land had been surveyed, it would usually be offered and sold at public auction as "offered lands." Until ceded land had been survey and offered for sale at auction, it was referred to as "unoffered lands."

Squatters, who were often short of cash, were at a disadvantage at public land auctions. Congress responded to this problem by passing a series of preemption laws for several specific geographical areas. These laws first entitled a squatter to preempt (that is, have the first opportunity to purchase) the land on which he had already settled. The Preemption Act of 1841 (see Appendix E) did not initially affect Florida since it was not a state until 1845. For a discussion of the Homestead Act of 1862 see Appendix F.

United States lands still vacant in Florida in 1890 was subject to entry by land warrants, by purchase, and by homestead entry and such lands were to be found in almost every township in the State.

However, settlers were warned that in the older settlements, where transportation facilities have been long enjoyed and the lands are of good quality, *very little, if any, vacant land can be found.* All inquiries as to Federal lands were to be addressed to Register United States Land Office, Gainesville, Florida.

The State Land Office was at Tallahassee. All inquires as to vacant state land was to be made there. A map showing the location of all vacant land in the state was not produced as it was deemed impractical as it would require daily revision. Prospective purchasers or homesteaders were directed to rely on their personal inspection and told to first find a piece of land that suited them, then ascertain if already owned or whether it was still in the public domain and owned by the Federal or State governments.

Like the Federal lands, few State land of any value or desirable quality was considered available for homesteading or purchase.

Prices of State Lands, 1890

School lands and Seminary lands are subject to entry at their appraised value, not less than $ 1.25 per acre. The larger portion of these lands is held at $ 1.25 per acre, but some tracts are valued as high as $ 7.00. Payment could be made either in United States currency or State scrip.

Internal Improvement lands generally at held at $ 1.25 per acre also, none less; some as high as $ 6.50 per acre payable in United States currency.
Swamp lands of forty acres could be had for $ 1.00 per acre, for more than forty but not exceeding eighty acres the price was 90 cents. For more than eighty and not exceeding two hundred acres, 80 cents; for more than two hundred acres but not more than 640 acres, 75 cents; for more than 640 acres, 70 cents per acre payable in United States currency.

In the case of entries of land at less than $ 1.00, the land could not be in detached pieces, but must lie in a body. Terms of sale in all cases were cash only. Lands could not be reserved from sale for the benefit of any applicant and an application not accompanied with the full amount of purchase money does not give any priority.

But by the act of March 7, 1881, " actual settlers upon any of the public lands of this State may enter the lands upon which they reside or have in cultivation, not to exceed 160 acres, to be taken in compact form according to the legal subdivisions, at the prices now or hereafter to be established for such lands, by paying one-third the purchase money at the time of the entry, one-third of the same within two years thereafter, and the remaining one-third within three years after the date of entry."

By the act of February 16, 1872, the right of homestead was given on the overflowed and swamp lands:

"Section 6: Any person who is the head of a family or who has arrived at the age of twenty-one years, and is a citizen of the United States, or who shall have filed his declaration of an intention to become such, as required by the laws of the United States, shall, from and after the first day of April, be entitled to enter one-quarter section, or a less quantity of the unsold swamp and overflowed lands granted to the State of Florida by act of Congress, approved 28th day of September, 1850. Any person, owning or residing on land may, under the provisions of sections six to thirteen of this chapter, enter other lands contiguous to his or her said land, which shall not, with the lands so already owned and occupied, exceed in the aggregate 160 acres".

"Section 7. The person applying for the benefit of section shall file with the Commissioner of Lands his or her affidavit that he or she is the head of a family, or is twenty-one years or more of age, and that such application is made for his or her exclusive use and benefit, and that the said entry is made for the purpose of actual settlement and cultivation, and not directly or indirectly for the use and benefit of any other person or persons whatsoever, and upon filing said affidavit with the Commissioner of Lands, and upon payment of ten dollars where the entry is more than eighty acres, and of five dollars where the entry is not of more than eighty acres, he or she shall thereupon be permitted to enter the amount of land specified; Provided however, that no deed shall issue therefore until the expiration of five years from the date of such entry; and if at the expiration of such time, or any time within two years thereafter the person making such entry, or, if he be dead, his widow, or, in case of her death, his heirs or devisees, or, in case of a widow making such entry, her heirs or devisees, in case of her death, shall prove by two credible witnesses that he, she or they have reclaimed said lands by means of levees and drains, and resided upon and cultivated the same for the term of five years immediately succeeding the time of filing the affidavit aforesaid, and shall make affidavit that no part of said land has been alienated; then, in such case, he, she or they shall be entitled to a deed."

Settlers who preferred railroad lands were directed to contact the various railroads directly where they could purchase the available land at prices and conditions set by those companies.

Pleasant Grove

Pleasant Grove was a farming community which came into being in 1878. A Post Office was established 3 March 1879 with Sarah J. Folks as Postmaster to serve the 48 families in the nearby area. She was replaced by Theresa Blitch 24 April 1880 and the PO was disestablished 15 June 1882. For location see Appendix G.

Blind Horse

The earliest known crossing location on the lower Withlacoochee River was called Blind Horse Crossing even before 1862. Long before ferries were constructed, this was the only way to get a horse or wagon across the river. It was located just below the Big Eddy, some two miles above the current US 19 bridge. Warren Paul moved his family from Crystal River in February 1862 to the Withlacoochee, locating on the south side (then Hernando County) of the crossing. The landing then became known as Paul's Landing. Paul lived here for several years. At the time there were just three roads from Crystal River: one to Homosassa, one to the lakes near present day Inverness and the third to Ocala which passed north crossing the river near Black Dirt, using Hodges Ferry (his first ferry).

So while southern Levy County was officially the Black Dirt District, and the first permanent white community was Black Dirt, the immediate area surrounding this crossing of the lower Withlacoochee River continued to be known as Blind Horse well into the 1890s.

The second ferry across the lower Withlacoochee River was known as Blitch's Ferry and was permitted by the Levy County Board of County Commissioners on June 1, 1885 (see Board of County Commission Book B, pages 257-258) with similar requirements and fees as set for Hodges Ferry (see page 59 for these rates). Mr. D. W. Blitch had first signed a letter of agreement to purchase the NW quarter of the NW quarter and the E one half of the NW quarter of Section 3 Township 17 and Range 17 in 1880 (this place was later the location of the Florida Power Inglis Steam Plant). By 1885 the area, years later to be known as Inglis, had grown sufficiently to create a demand for a better river crossing as it was very much out of the way to travel further downriver to Hodges Ferry (the second one located near present day Izaak Walton Lodge). Mr. Blitch determined to build a ferry and sought county permission to charge the public for conveyance.

Typical ferry of the period courtesy of Florida State Archives Photo Collection.

When white pioneers first arrived in Levy County, there were numerous Indian trails leading from village to village and from villages to hunting or fishing locations. Over the course of time these Indians would have learned of the possible locations to ford the river and thus that is where the trails would lead. From Hampton Dunn's book, *A History of Citrus County*, we learn that Blind Horse Crossing (notice "crossing" not "ferry") was in use prior to 1862. This natural ford of the river is located just below the "Big Eddy", some 2 miles up river from the current US 19 bridge. The original road from the Inglis area to Crystal River utilized this crossing of the river and is shown on early maps and drawings. This crossing in later years came to be known as Harrison's Ford, being so called for a family who settled nearby on the north bank, while the south side was called Paul's Landing for the family living there.

At the location of the present dam there was a shoal and natural bottle-neck. The lower river perhaps experienced a greater tidal affect than it currently does. At low tides this crossing was easily made by a man walking or on horseback and indeed even a wagon. There are normally two low tides in 24 hours with one usually being much lower than the other, the depth of water being dependent on the moon's location. Sometimes the low tide would occur during daylight hours and be of sufficient magnitude to drop the water to a depth where crossing was possible. Thus the river could be forded once a day at the most, but even then, not all days in a month. We know that most early movement of merchandise and goods was by boat. Again we learn from Hampton Dunn's *History of Citrus County* that goods bound for Ocala were shipped by boat from the port at Cedar Key to Crystal River where they were moved by wagon to a ferry crossing near where present day SR200 crosses the Withlacoochee. With the buildup of the Inglis area a demand was created for a better crossing of the river and thus the demand for a ferry was finally realized by 1885.

Old-timers that tell stories of Blind Horse Ferry are simply not old enough to have ever actually seen such a ferry. So their stories are based on second or third hand information and hearsay. Despite their belief that their stories are factual, we must consider where they got their alleged "facts". The several stories one hears of a blind horse pulling a ferry or that a blind horse fell off a ferry thus giving the ferry the name Blind Horse Ferry, are ridiculous.

It is easy to see how Blind Horse Crossing, an early whiteman's name for the ford over time became confused with nearby Blitch's Ferry and thus was born the myth of Blind Horse Ferry, which in fact was Blitch's Ferry.

Typical ferry of the period courtesy of Florida State Archives Photo Collection.

Lebanon (Hoke Johnson)

The community of Lebanon began in the 1870s as a farming area, later it would be active in logging and turpentine with its own short line railroad line from Dunnellon. There is some indication that the area was first known as "Hoke Johnson". No doubt this was due early settler Hasten H. "Hoke" Johnson who purchased land here in July 1872. Christopher Columbus Gaines (called Lum) was another early prominent settler, moving to the area from Citrus County with his new bride Frances Barco, shortly after their marriage on 29 December 1870. Born in South Carolina, Lum Gaines moved to Florida where he served in the 3rd Seminole Indian War, Florida State Militia in 1862-3 and Confederate Infantry 9th Regiment from June 1864 to the end of the war.

The story is often told of how Gaines delivered the mail to his neighbors for a year before a Post Office was finally established in his general store on 3 October 1889 with him as the Post Master to serve the 50 families located nearby. It would continue in operation until his death in 1923. In addition to his store and large farm were the general store of Stephen Swep Robinson and the Holder Turpentine Company's still. Additionally there was a sawmill, church and school. Lebanon was located on the old wagon road from Bronson to Blind Horse Crossing, see Appendix G.

The author's Great-Grandfather was Swepston B. W. Stephens who moved near the Seminole Agency at Fort King in 1846 with his step-father, Lewis C. Gaines. A few years ago while doing genealogy research I came across the name Christopher C. Gaines of Lebanon and suspected they might be related. With so many other clues and trails to follow, I haven't yet pursued this one but I have discovered that Lum Gaines' son Ernest married Cely Elkins who was my father's sister-in-law. So while there is probably a distant blood relationship on the Gaines side, we have confirmed this marriage connection.

During one of my visits with my 92 year young mother Betty Sims in 2005, I mentioned reading one of the books by Citrus resident Judge E. C. May. I was surprised to hear my mother say she had known the Judge! You see, mother came to Florida from her native Georgia in 1939 to teach school at the Yankeetown High School. After marrying my father in 1940, they moved to Dunnellon. After a few years teaching high school, they needed a 6th grade teacher and she was recruited but after a year she moved down to the 4th grade where she remained for many years. One of the requirements was the teaching of Florida History and mother sought to make it more interesting by learning local area history herself and also to invite local citizens to her classroom who could tell firsthand tales of the phosphate boom and frontier Florida. Judge E. C. May had come up from Inverness and opened a store in Dunnellon in 1898, so not only was he a great storyteller, but he had firsthand knowledge of the situation. Mother never knew of our blood relationship to the family of Christopher Gaines so imagine my surprise when I recently learned that Judge May and Christopher Gaines had been friends! Lebanon is now a ghost town with nothing left but the Cedars of Lebanon Cemetery, but from the mid 1880s until the 1930s it was a busy place with stores, school, church, Post Office and a reported 50 families in residence. By the 1950s the town had faded away and the cemetery was in deplorable condition. Concerned citizens and descendants of those lying in peaceful rest got together to put the cemetery back into shape. The following is a story written by Judge E. C. May of that event and is reprinted here as it was written:

Judge May as a young man.

Cedars of Lebanon Cemetery   by Judge E. C. May

" November 25, 1956, I spent three pleasant hours with a gathering at the Cedars of Lebanon Cemetery, near the town of Lebanon, in Levy County, where neighbors, friends and relatives were gathered to lovingly clean up this historic spot and put it in the good shape in which we found it.

I am told that for many years the place had been neglected and had grown up in weeds and small trees, as far too many such places are neglected when the old are gone and buried there, and the young have married, moved away and acquired other interests which make them forget.

One of the daughters of Columbus Gaines, Mrs. I. D. Wingate of Inverness, was the prime mover, and did much work in getting this old cemetery cleaned up.

When it was established many years ago, the land was covered by great cedar trees for which Columbus Gaines named the place, but in later years in its forlorn and neglected state, a great woods fire destroyed them and now few remain.

This place has much interesting history, some of which I know, and many of my old friends and acquaintances are buried there, in addition to Columbus Gaines and his wife, Frances Barco, and Frank Allen, a peace officer who was killed by another officer, a Negro deputy sheriff.

This was an unfortunate accident. Both officers were looking for a Negro murderer when they met on the railroad bridge at Dunnellon in the darkness and both thought they had met their man!

They shot it out and before they discovered their mistake both were dead, each riddled by the other's bullets. This is one of the tragic stories of the old days which I hope to write some day.

When I moved my store to Dunnellon in February 1898, as told in my book, *Gaters, Skeeters and Malary,* Lum Gaines became my customer and friend, and for many years I knew him well.

I met several of his daughters at the cemetery—Mrs. Leona Gaines Oglesby of 509 Norfolk Circle, Lakeland; Mrs. I. D. Wingate who lives near me in Inverness, and Mrs. Williams of Cotton Plant. We stood together with bowed heads at the tomb of their parents in this old cemetery and recalled many pleasant memories of those illustrious pioneers and their long useful lives.

At the call for dinner we walked out of that sacred place into the nearby woods, where a feast fit for royalty was served to 100 guests. After dinner the people sang the old and inspiring hymns of the days of Lum and Frances Gaines, and several of those present made short addresses.

Columbus Gaines was born in South Carolina and came to Florida with his brother when he was 14 years old. His family were all dead, and when his brother returned to his home, Columbus decided to stay. He was then on his own, and he joined the army and fought at Fort Clinch (in Levy County during the 2nd Seminole Indian War).

When the war was over he got a job at the sawmill on Chambers Island which is now Port Inglis. He rafted logs on the Withlacoochee and did other common labor and saved his money.

When he was 18 and she was 17, he married Frances Barco, the daughter of the owner of the big Barco plantation at Blitch's Ferry.

She was a sister of Nick Barco, who for many years was prominent in business and politics in Citrus County. Among his other activities he operated a sawmill at Crystal River for many years with Mr. Blanton, under the trade name of Barco & Blanton, and he served several terms as Treasurer of Citrus County. Many of the children and other relatives of those men still live in Florida, and some in Citrus County.

Soon after their marriage December 29, 1870, Lum and Frances Gaines located in Levy County and established their home and farm at what is now Lebanon, where they lived out their lives and raised their 12 children, one adopted child and two orphans.

Lum Gaines established the first church in his territory, hauling the lumber many miles from the sawmill at Parkersburg in an ox wagon, and although he was not an ordained minister he often preached there on Sunday. He was a justice of the peace and held court when there was anything to do, and was also a notary public. He married many couples and officiated at funerals. He established this old cemetery and saw to it that it was well kept as long as he lived.

Five main roads converged on Lebanon Church, and it was well attended. There were no automobiles in those days and people came by wagon, horseback, ox cart and on foot from many miles around, and it was not unusual to see 50 carts and wagons gathered there and more than 300 people come to worship. The old church house stood until recent years and was destroyed by fire of unknown origin.

Photo from the author's collection.

In time Mr. Gaines induced the government to establish a post office, which he named Lebanon, inspired by the forest of great cedar trees which covered the land and from the Bible story of the Cedars of Lebanon from which Hiram, King of Tyre, furnished King Solomon the timber to build his temple.

Lum Gaines was named postmaster by President Grant in 1870 and served continuously under 13 presidents from Grant to Coolidge, 10 of whom were Republicans. Many people tried to get the office with no success and when he died in 1923 the office was abandoned and the territory is now served by R. F. D. from Dunnellon. In order to get the post office in the first place Mr. Gaines carried the mail "outside" in an ox wagon for a whole year free. He did not even get stamp cancellation, and in later years he never got more.

Being postmaster at Lebanon was never profitable but Lum Gaines thought little of money. He made his living on his farm and was ever ready to work for nothing if it helped his neighbors or served the interest of the community.

It is my understanding that the postal authorities have a rule which prevents anyone from serving more than 50 years as postmaster. Lum Gaines served continuously for 54 years and so far as I know established a record for long service (Editor's note: the 54 years is an obvious error, apparently Judge Mays was misinformed).

The only other person I ever heard of who served nearly so many years was Charles A. Miller, who served as postmaster at Fairmont, in west Citrus County until the railroads came and that office was abandoned. He was then appointed postmaster for Crystal River and served until recent years, when this rule forced his retirement.

It is a coincidence that Cliff Gaines, a son of Lum Gaines, married Nellie Miller, a daughter of Charles A. Miller.

Lum Gaines was a living example of the best of rural life in the old South, which is now little more that a memory. He was more than a citizen. He became an institution around which the life of the settlement revolved.

That was not unusual in those far-off days. In most isolated settlements one man would rise to leadership and his word and example carried great weight. This seldom paid off in money and there was plenty of free work to do and plenty of free meals to serve to those who came for help or advice and stayed for dinner, and often until the next day, with no thought of pay. Such men seldom had a thought beyond the welfare of his neighbors and his community.

Such a man was Columbus Gaines, and his wife, Frances Barco, stood by his side and did her part.

The work and example of that pioneer couple will be a power for good in their children and those to follow long after their names are forgotten. It is still true that in free America a man makes his life anything he wants it to be."

Another early settler was John Boothy Robinson who immigrated to America from England with a brother. He married Miss Caroline E. Raulerson in Levy County in 1867 and they had four boys and a girl (Cass Elliot, Horace Boothy, Stephen Swep, Moses Elias and Eliza Ann). He initially settled near the Withlacoochee River east of the old community of Black Dirt, but soon his children settled in Lebanon Station and Lebanon. Son Stephen Swep Robinson (named for Swepston "Swep" B. W. Stephens) operated a general store at Lebanon for many years.

This picture shows the old Robinson home place at Lebanon ca. . John and Caroline Robinson are in the buggy on the right. Cass is the small boy standing in front of the buggy with sister Eliza. Photo courtesy of Louise Robinson Smith.

Son Cass Elliot Robinson married Josephine "Josie" Stephens, daughter of another early settler, Isham C. Stephens and Elizabeth K. Jones, in 1901. They had two boys and a girl, Elliot Elizabeth, Isham John and Nelson Cass.

Nelson Cass, Isham John and Eliot Elizabeth Robinson, she has just started school. Ca. 1908. Photo courtesy of Louise Robinson Smith.

Tragedy struck the family in 1908 when Josephine was doing the laundry one afternoon. The ground-length skirt of her dress caught fire and she died.

Robinson family oral history tells us that the Stephens family donated the land for the Cedars of Lebanon Cemetery, even suggesting that this burial actually established the cemetery, and it was thus named by C. C. Gaines who probably performed the burial rites for Josie, as he often served as minister. Although a lovely story, much of it is fiction.

Josephine with her parents Isham C. Stephens and Elizabeth Jones. Photo courtesy of Louise Robinson Smith.

Josephine Stephens Robinson shortly before her death. Photo courtesy of Louise Robinson Smith.

Common to that time, a community church (single story frame structure) was built in a convenient location and also used two or three months of the year for a school. After a few years, when the church became formally established with elected officials, they determined to obtain legal ownership of the property. A deed was thus obtained by the original church trustees, C. C. Gaines, William H. Stephens, Robert King, Isham C. Stephens, Jonas Driggers, W. H. Dias and James M. Stephens. The land was donated by partners E. J. Lutterloh and Horatio Davis on 10 October 1890. We cannot be certain exactly when the church and school was established, but we can be certain it was as early as October 1886 when Benjamin F. Beesman, a young man of 31 years was buried in the church yard. No one by this name (or any variation of the name) is found in the census of 1885 or later, so exactly who he was and what his story was is lost to history.

The earliest ceremony of record in the church was the marriage of C. C. Gaines' daughter, Miss F. C. Gaines on September 26, 1895 to W. C. Blanton of Citronelle (in Citrus County). Officiating was Reverend E. A. Harrison with Groomsmen Horace Robinson and Dock McKee and Bridesmaids Leona Gaines (sister of the bride) and Malinda Coleman. Entertainment was provided by the schoolteacher Professor Chaney.

In later years the Cedars of Lebanon Cemetery Fund and later the Cedars of Lebanon Cemetery Association, Inc. would be established to care and preserve this historic place. These organizations would eventually receive deeded ownership of the original church and burial property and in 1997 would purchase an additional 2.66 acres on the west and south sides from the State of Florida, doubling the size. Burial is open to long-time residents of the area and relatives of those pioneers already interred.

Lebanon Station

This community north of Lebanon began as a stop on the Atlantic Coastline Railroad. The exact date of its beginning is lost to history but it dates from the early 1900s and it survived well into the 1950s. The only reason for the stop on the railroad was the need to load dolomite from the nearby quarry of the Dixie Lime Company. Soon homes for the workers had been constructed which led to a few stores and later a filling station (gasoline).

With nearby Tidewater and Lebanon providing services, a post office was never established here.

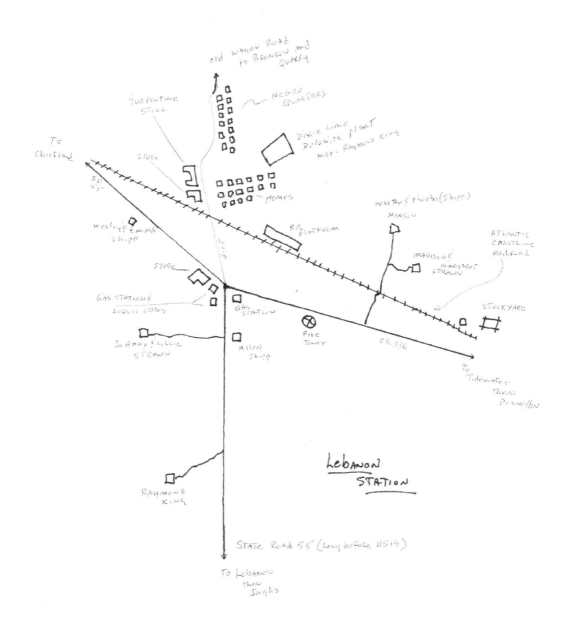

Old Wagon Road to Bronson and Quarry

Turpentine Still

Negro Quarters

Dixie Lime Plant
Dolomite Plant
mgr - Raymond King

To Chiefland

Store

Homes

Westry & Emma Shipp

Walter & Phoebe (Shipp)

Mixon

R.R. Platform

Atlantic Coastline Railroad

Madison & Margaret Strawn

Store

Stockyard

Gas Station & Liquor Store

Gas Station

Johnny & Lillie Strawn

Allen Shipp

Fire Tower

C.R. 336

To Tidewater Then Dunnellon

Raymond King

Lebanon Station

State Road 55 (long before US19)

To Lebanon Then Inglis

Albertus Vogt and Phosphate

Phosphate had been found in Florida as early as 1868 as recorded by Dr. N. A. Pratt, of South Carolina, when he discussed Florida having phosphate in his studies of the mineral. During the opening of a stone quarry in

Hawthorne, Florida, about 1879, low-grade phosphate was again discovered. In 1881, Capt. John Francis LeBaron of the Army Engineers reported finding pebble phosphate in the Peace River near the town of Arcadia. Interestingly, he was conducting a survey in search of a route for a proposed canal from the head waters of the St. Johns River to Charlotte Harbor! So clearly it is not exactly true that Vogt "discovered" phosphate in Florida as has so often been written, and technically he didn't even "discover" it when it was found near Dunnellon.

Vogt was an interesting character and lived an adventurous life. In 1870 we find 20 year old Albertus living at Camp Izard in Marion County with his Uncle Dr. Daniel Vogt and other family members. No occupation is given for him, probably due to his still recovering from wounds received during the recent Civil War and his Uncle being financially successful. He had been born in South Carolina at Ashland Plantation, St. Mathews Parish, Orangeburg District on 8 April 1850. When the Civil War broke out in 1861 he was just eleven years old. By 1864, when he was the ripe old age of 14 and the Confederacy was desperate for manpower, he was attending the Prep School of Carlisle Beeman and William J. Northern at Mount Zion, Georgia. On 23 August 1864 his father was mortally wounded at Chestnut Ridge near Atlanta. He was sent by special train to Mayfield, Georgia and thence to his Sunny Side Plantation three miles away where he died that night and was buried at Horeb Cemetery near Mayfield. So it was that young Vogt left school and enlisted at Sunny Side Plantation, in General Joseph E. Wheeler's Cavalry, Company F, 12th Regiment and went direct to Camak, Waren County, Georgia, engaging there in a skirmish with a body of Stoneman's Cavalry which was destroying the railroad. In the hand to hand combat, Vogt was wounded by a saber cut to his left forearm and the left side of his head. That night he was sent with other wounded to the hospital at Millidgeville, Ga.

After about three weeks of recovery, he rejoined his company at Midway, Georgia and proceeded to Jeffersonville, Twiggs County, Georgia, where they again skirmished with a detachment of Yankee Cavalry and he was again wounded and his little mare "Nellie" was killed from under him. Thus he returned once again to the hospital at Millidgeville.

Many people believe the Civil War ended at the surrender of General Lee at Appomattox Courthouse, Va. General Lee, in fact only surrendered the army under his command, the Army of Northern Virginia. While the war was effectually over, it in fact was not technically over as the General had no authority to surrender the South. By this time the need for manpower was so desperate that even the wounded were required to leave their hospital beds. Vogt and others were ordered to Andersonville Prison where they were used as guards so others in better physical shape could be released to fight.

About this time it became clear to the Confederate leadership that the cause was lost. As the Yankees had threatened to hang them as traitors, President Jefferson Davis and the other Confederate Cabinet Officers determined to escape from the country. By this time the only direction available was south and hopefully by blockade runner from Florida. Yankee General Wilson at Macon ordered numerous detachments to scour the countryside for the Confederate leaders. Learning this information, Captain Woerz at Andersonville ordered Vogt and as many others as could ride to intercept and guerilla fight any Yankees. Vogt would later report his last orders from Captain Woerz as,

"Boys, you will not take any prisoners, not one, nor will you surrender under any circumstances – if you take a prisoner, you will have no place to deliver him – you can't keep him, for if he escapes, your whereabouts and numbers will immediately be betrayed, and that would be suicidal. If they capture you, you will certainly be hanged; stampede and capture their horses and all other live stock they may be driving – report to me by courier whenever possible; hang or shoot every Federal scout you meet, for they are spies. Andersonville will be captured very soon; ambush the raiders and destroy them – good-bye and good luck to you."

Acting Sergeant Vogt and his small group established a rendezvous at Lake Fernside in Brooks County, Georgia, between Quitman and the Florida line. It was while here that they learned of the capture of President Davis and the surrender of Generals Lee and Johnston. Vogt and the others decided to disperse and return to their various homes, thus they were never captured nor were they paroled by the Yankees.

Following his Civil War exploits he went west as did many of his companions. We find no records of this period and although he was a somewhat prolific writer and storyteller, he makes no mention of where he went or what his adventures where. He would reappear in Florida in the 1870 census as we previously said and he would be a US Marshal, engineer, Ocala-Homosassa stagecoach operator, journalist and world traveler.

Albertus' brothers and sisters had been separated upon their father's death in 1864. Older brother Sydney was reared by an uncle, Dr. Frederick Vogt, in South Carolina. Sister Elizabeth Roxanne was reared by her mother's brother, John H. Walker, in Georgia. Brother John Walker Vogt was reared by Uncle Jacob Vogt, who owned a cotton and cane plantation in Marion County, Florida, and was a teacher at East Florida Seminary in Ocala. John would live with Uncle Jake, a widower, and several cousins until about 1876, when Jacob died. John at this time is eighteen and on his own. Albertus' guardian was to have been his Uncle Dr. Daniel Vogt with whom he is found living in 1870.

As brothers, John and Albertus began to spend much time together and became good friends. They seemed to have a special bond, although quite unlike in personality. Both were energetic and hard-working, and about 1885 the two became equal partners in the real estate business, opening an office in Ocala. When Albertus made the discovery of hard-rock phosphate on his home place, their lives were changed, yet the two remained partners in business and best friends.

Settling on the north bank of the Withlacoochee River near a clear water spring on land he purchased from Renfro, he expected to grow citrus. He lived very "high" and came to be called the "Duke of Dunnellon".

Vogt circa 1885 just before the phosphate boom. Photo courtesy of Vogt descendant David Duval.

Vogt's servant, old black Tom, was working in the yard when he uncovered some large bones and material later identified as highly concentrated phosphate. He became quite scared at the bones and brought the material to the attention of his boss. Vogt loaded the material in a barrel and placed it in his buggy. Taking it around Dunnellon for all to see, no one could identify what it was. He then proceeded to take it to Ocala; again no one could identify the material. Finally he sent it off for assaying and was told it was phosphate. Armed with this information, he proceeded to purchase all the land he could afford before the word of his discovery leaked out. Unfortunately his actions had already informed the populace the land boom was on!

Unfortunately Vogt decided to sell early in the boom of land prices, half of all his holdings being bought by John F. Dunn, an Ocala banker. The other half he sold for some $200,000.

From an article written by Albertus in June 28, 1889 entitled *Life in Florida* we read:

The Withlacoochee

The water-lily dips its vase of snow
On many a shallow cove along whose graceful edge the purple flowers grow
And dappled river beds and tufted sedge,
And in the stream beneath their image lies
Mirrored like beauty in a lover's eyes.

Almost immediately on the 29th parallel of latitude, there empties into the Mexico Gulf one of the most weird, romantic and beautiful of American Rivers. On account of its strong current flowing at least five miles an hour, making it's ascent in a row-boat is full of pulling, but with my good darkies, Tom and Paddie, at the oars, my Winchester for 'gators, my Parker's gun for water-fowl, and our old dogs, Hamp and Vie, for game; when in camp along the banks, a stout bamboo pole and phantom minnows for bobbing, 100 feet of line, and a tiny spool hook for trolling, with my very estimable wife for company, a bottle of Augustova &c. for tonic and scoring, we've made, probably, the most pleasurable of the many trips of our lives, up the ever-changing, always tolling, suggestive waters of our beloved Withlacoochee.

To reach the gulf we drive from our home near Dunnellon, 18 miles across a sparsely settled country to the winter home of our friends, the Alldays, who have purchased "Bonita Island" from the estate of Dr. Hodges, who knew a good thing when he saw it, and who here built one of the most conveniently appointed of the three homes in which he lived, accumulating a competency and enjoying it like a white man. Rev. C. A. Allday, on the strength of his bordering blonde beauty, wedded an Alabama fortune, invested a part of it here and is living after the Hodge fashion.......He keeps a fair pack of hounds, some good guns, and in the proper season kills a few deer, varying the fun by gratuitous preaching in the rural settlements around, where with a voice a half-mile square, he wakes up the natives.

In the creation of Mrs. Allday, nature was working on an intensive system and put all the good possible into her make-up. Generous, brainy, accomplished, domestic, and with a voice like Neilson's, she forces us to the conclusion that while her "marriage is not a failure", her choice of domestic life has robbed the world of a song queen. After an evening of charming music, and being subjected to an antiquated order of camp meeting prayer, compressed into a room 18 feet square, with a 12 foot ceiling, rushing out and up until if flows through the top of a 35 foot chimney.

We turned in to rest........It is morning. We are up early-eight o'clock breakfast is perfect. Oysters not five minutes out of the water, "any way you want 'em", venison steak, fish, rice, sliced tomatoes, cukes with the dew on and onions white as snow, a charming hostess and our prayerful, parson-sportsman; metamorphosed into the most jovial of hosts – as full of jest and frolic as a sixteen year old, not withstanding his while hair and 49 years.

Vogt had married the widow Mary Renfro Anderson and built his mansion Rosebank (which is still standing as this book goes to press) just prior to the phosphate discovery.

His brother John had met Margaret Vassie in Dunnellon, where she was a school teacher. They were married by a Methodist minister in Dunnellon in 1889. Their first home was on Bonita Island, where their daughter Adelaide Bonita, was born in 1890, and their son, William Vassie, was born in 1892, and the adjacent creek would come to be known as Vassie Creek although the name is often misspelled on current maps as Vassey.

Soon after William was born, John moved his family into the beautiful new home that he had designed and built for them in Levy County, about nine miles west of Albertus' and Mary's home. John Walker Vogt, Jr. was the first of their children to be born in this new home in 1894. In 1897, a daughter, Marguerite was born, but lived only two weeks. A son, Kenneth Leonidas, was born in 1899, but he only lived ten months.

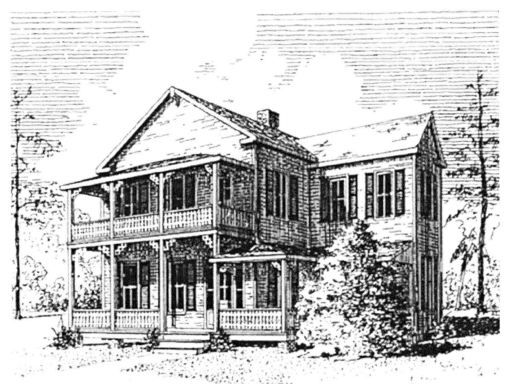

"Sunnyside", John Walker Vogt, Sr.'s Levy County home. Sketch courtesy of Vogt descendant David Duval.

About 1900, John Walker Vogt, Sr., became ill. His illness was diagnosed as a kidney ailment, then called Bright's disease. For almost two years John suffered before dying August 11, 1901, at age 43.

Albertus had lost his brother, his best friend and now knew he had sold out his holdings too soon, leaving him very depressed. Selling his remaining holdings and Rosebank, he moved to Polk County near Bartow where he again got into the real estate business. His reputation would be smeared when he was charged with trying to sell land as oil bearing when drums of oil are found buried on the site.

Albertus would leave Bartow and his land troubles and move to Jacksonville where he died December 12, 1921. His remains would be returned to Ocala where a large funeral was held.

Captain John Livingston Inglis

The next prominent citizen we will discuss was born in Liverpool, England of Scotch parents. Much has been written about Inglis, and as with Hodges, much is wrong. This author is fortunate to possess a rare copy of a manuscript by Sara May Love, grand-daughter to Inglis. I am indebted to Inglis descendant and genealogy researcher, Kay Inglis Bachman for this manuscript and other information about this important Levy County Pioneer.

Sara writes: *My mother was Louise Inglis, the only daughter of John L. Inglis. When I was a little girl and didn't want to go to bed, she would lie down by me and tell me a story about "when she was a little girl." She had four brothers and they lived a little way out of Madison* (Florida).

John Livingston Inglis was born 1 January 1837 to Andrew Inglis and Sarah Livingston. Andrew was by occupation an engineer. Andrew had been educated at the grammar school in West Cowes, Isle of Wight, and as a very young man he came to Philadelphia in 1857, where he was apprenticed to a steel works. John had come to this country with his aunt, Mag Townsend. She first brought him to Madison, Florida, to meet his Livingston relatives and then he went back to Philadelphia where he worked for three years. He then traveled to St. Marks Florida where he was to install a sawmill. While there the Civil War broke out. He sympathized with his southern cousins so he went in on the southern side. He enlisted as a private in the Wakulla Guards at Newport, Florida and his company was initially stationed at Fort Williams at the mouth of the St. Marks River. Later he was assigned to the 2nd Florida Regiment, rising in rank to Captain. His service in the war ended at the battle of Nashville in December 1864 when he was captured. He was then held until the end of the war at Johnson's Island, Ohio.

Captain John L. Inglis in 1867. Photo courtesy of Florida State Archives photo collection.

Following the war, John's father Andrew had established himself in partnership with Samuel B. Thomas and Archie Livingston (a relative) in Madison, in what would become the principal Sea Island cotton gin in the South for many years (Author's note: Sea Island cotton grows only near the coast and has much longer fibers than regular cotton. It also has one large seed pod rather than numerous small seeds.) The company was known as the Florida Manufacturing Company. In August 1866, Andrew Inglis had signed articles of agreement with two local merchants for the company. The stated purpose was to carry out saw milling, grist milling and cotton ginning. Andrew apparently was the mastermind of this venture as he was a construction engineer, millwright and machinist. Thomas and Livingston *were the moneymen. Andrew designed the plant and superintended the operation. He was to receive a salary of $1,000 annually and one third of the profits. Unfortunately, Andrew died a year after the agreement was signed and it is doubtful that the cotton gin was completed before his death.*

John had married the daughter of his father's partner, Louisa "Miss Lou" Thomas on 17 November 1869 and they had seven children: Beattie Andrew, John L. Jr. (died as a baby), Louise Thomas, Allick Wyllie, William Lawtey, Andrew (also died young) and Edgar Auchincloss.

Inglis family photo courtesy of Inglis descendant Kay Inglis Bachman.

These children were all educated in such schools as there were in Madison, Florida at the time. Beattie attended first the Citadel, then Stevens Tech in New Jersey. Louise Thomas attended Agnes Scott which at the time was called The Institute. Allick and Lawt both went to V.M.I., but graduated from Georgia Tech. Edgar attended Vanderbilt.

Beatie while at the Citadel. Photo courtesy of Inglis descendant Kay Inglis Bachman.

Lawtey, photo courtesy of Inglis descendant Kay Inglis Bachman.

John Inglis had at least one sister, Marianne, who married Allick Wyllie. Allick came to Florida several times from his home in Scotland and invested in the phosphate business. John Inglis' brother Robert fought on "the other side" in the Civil War and settled later in Wisconsin where he was a Customs Officer.

Miss Lou's family was very close. Her mother was Keziah William Brinson and she married Samuel Beatty Thomas. They had migrated from Thomas County Georgia to Madison County Florida in a wagon with one child, Frank, and one little slave girl.

97

Miss Lou had two sisters, Big Auntie (Jane) and Little Auntie (Ashton) and there were at least two brothers, one being Frank. He married Sally Ardis, the daughter of the preacher and they had Anna. Sally died in childbirth and Grandmother Thomas took her to raise saying that when Frank married again he would have a big family and they would make Anna the nursemaid! Jane married Chandler Smith and they had a son who died a teenager and a daughter Audrey, who married Jim Sharon and lived in Quincy.

Little Auntie (Ashton) never married and when her parents died she came to live with Miss Lou and John Inglis. Grandfather provided her a job at the Florida Manufacturing Company, thus she was the first woman to go to work in an office in Madison.

John Inglis gave his wife lovely jewelry. She had an amethyst and pearl necklace and pin which she always wore and several diamonds. He would purchase this jewelry in New York on his many business trips, especially after he got into business with Ralph Barker and Edgar Auchincloss who had offices there.

I cannot honestly say what church affiliation John Inglis had but I would guess Scotch Presbyterian. The Thomases (sic) were Baptist. Big Auntie taught the Sunbeams at the Baptist Church for many years and all the children attended. Beatty was a deacon in Riverside Baptist Church in Jacksonville, Louise, a staunch Baptist, taught Sunday School for years and was president of the W.M.U. in Quincy. Allick was an elder and for many years Treasurer of Riverside Presbyterian Church in Jacksonville. Lawt wa an elder in the North Avenue Presbyterian Church in Atlanta and Edgar attended an Episcopalian Church in Miami.

When the Confederate Reunion was held in Jacksonville in 1914, Captain Inglis invited his old friends from his first company to come and stay at his home on Riverside. He also asked his son-in-law, Meade, to come and help for, as he said, "Some of them have never seen a flush toilet and others will get so drunk that they won't be able to get their boots off to go to bed!" Captain Inglis was elected General at this reunion and some 60,000 are said to have attended (actually he was elected Commander of the Florida Division of the United Confederate Veterans).

Unitied Confederate Veterans parade in Jacksonville, Florida in 1914. Capt. Inglis is the rider with the grey beard to the left in the lead. Photo courtesy of Florida State Archive photo collection.

John Inglis lived in Marion County during the heyday of phosphate but often visited Port Inglis and built a home on the island. He later moved to Jacksonville before 1904. He was a member of the New York Yacht Club and used his several yachts (all called Tuna) for entertaining his many friends and business associates. The yachts were generally kept at Jacksonville, but often sailed to New York and Port Inglis.

In the early 1900s he became acquainted with Frank Harris, editor of the Ocala Daily Banner, a newspaper. The following is excerpts from an article written by Harris of an adventure with Inglis.

A Cruise with Capt. Inglis.

In order to catch a whiff of the sea and a surcease from the maelstrom of political foul air that is generated by the "initiative referendum and recall," the editor of this paper accepted an invitation from Capt. John L. Inglis for a few days' cruise on the gulf of Mexico aboard his elegant new yacht, the "Tuna".

In Company with Judge W. S. Bullock we left Ocala on Thursday morning at 6:40 on board the "Sunny Allick" (train). We were met at Dunnellon by Mr. Allick Inglis, and were taken to Rockwell in his automobile.

Rockwell is only a few miles distant, and is the headquarters of the Dunnellon Phosphate Company. It is the parent company, and has witnessed the "rise and fall" of many rival companies. Incidents cluster about it as interesting as a romance and in his leisure moments Capt. Inglis could not do a better thing than to write a history of it (but he didn't!).

At Rockwell we boarded the Standard-Hernando Railroad train and were taken to Inglis, a distance of fifteen miles.

Railroad roundhouse and terminal at Rockwell, near present day Dunnellon. Photo courtesy of Florida State Archives Photo Collection.

This photo shows the railroad near its terminus in Inglis just west of Barker Chemical Company and just downstream of the Commissary building that was located near present day US 19 bridge. Photo from author's collection.

We found a ballasted road – the only one in Florida – and it is being put in elegant shape.

At Inglis are located the Dunnellon Drying Plant and the Barker Chemical Works. The Dunnellon Company crushes and dries all of its rock before shipping it. This renders it more valuable and gives a larger employment to labor. The Barker Chemical Works reduce the crude rock into sulfuric acid, and so far as we know it is the only plant of the kind in Florida.

Port Inglis is nine miles from Inglis. We were met there by Mr. R. A. Alfred in his little racing boat, the "Berenice". We covered the distance from Inglis to Port Inglis in twenty-three minutes.

Port Inglis is located on what was once known as Chambers Island and is the prettiest of the many little isles fringing the gulf. It juts well out to deep water, and commands a fine view of the famed Mexic (sic) sea.

On the most elevated spot Capt Inglis has erected an elegant bungalow, and here enjoys the soft gulf breezes and the luxuries of its delicacies. Besides he has a garden in which is growing a variety of spring vegetables and we saw on peach trees no larger than one's thumb, a most ambitious yield of promising fruit. It is also home to the fig. The fruit is most delicious and the leaves are large and lustrous, and we could not help thinking how Eve would have been delighted with them...

The Bungalow photo from the Author's collection.

After inspecting the grounds we were conducted aboard the "Tuna". It is the third yacht of the same name that Capt. Inglis has built....it is a fraction less than one hundred feet long and is about twenty feet in width. It was built at Baltimore from blue prints drawn under Capt. Inglis' supervision so everything is finished just as he wanted.....

The inside finishings (sic) are all of mahogany and the outside of teek (sic), a tree of the East Indies. The sides proper are of yellow pine. The chinaware, silverware and glassware are of the latest designs. The coat of arms – a diamond I – and the name of the Tuna are burned in the chinaware, engraved upon the silver and ground into the glassware. She is furnished with two bath and toilet rooms and one can enjoy hot or cold water baths with either fresh or salt water.

The Tuna carries two engines of 125 h.p. and is supplied with 1500 gallons of gasoline. It has a dynamo and storage batters and is capable of being brilliantly illuminated. Her crew consists of a captain, an engineer, a steward, a chef and a deckhand...

The yacht Tuna photo courtesy of Charles Brooker collection.

The Tuna has the Union Jack, the flag of the New York Yacht Club, Capt. Inglis' private flag and the Stars and Stripes all floating from her masts...

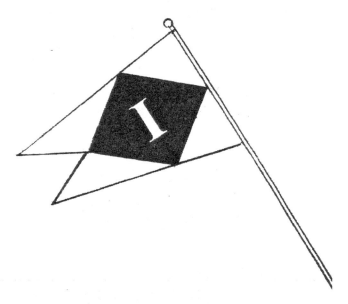

Capt. Inglis' private yacht flag.

....We immediately made out to sea, and in a few hours cast anchor off Cedar Key. Capt. Inglis was one of its pioneer citizens, erecting three large sawmills there and told an interesting tale of how the town waxed and waned. It was literally strangled to death by the short-sided policy pursued by those who owned the land, the same as Fernandina was on the Atlantic side, whose destiny happened to lay in the same hands. The owners would only lease...refusing to sell on any terms. Though having well the start and both possessing better harbors, the two cities saw Jacksonville and Tampa steal trade away from them so completely that Cedar Key, at least, remains but a relic of former times.

We soon raised anchor and again steamed away and spent the first night at the mouth of the historic Suwannee River. Bright and early the following morning we got an array of fishing tackle and lowered the launches and started out to interview the denizens of the deep.....The next morning the captain of the Tuna got up early and brought back any quantity of stone crabs and we had fish in all forms and varieties....

Capt. Inglis, on right, with fishing companions. Photo courtesy of Charles Brooker collection.

The next day we did more fishing and continued the fish diet with undiminished, if not increased, ardor, and cast anchor for the night at the entrance to Crystal River, off Shell Island. The next morning we leisurely steamed up to the headwaters of this translucid (sic) stream, where we disembarked in time to catch the train, which landed us at home for an Easter Dinner....

...Capt. Inglis...is an Englishman by birth, but was born of Scottish parents. He came when quite a young man to the United States, in 1857, and landed at Newport, Florida, now an extinct town, in 1860, so he is a southerner by preference and adoption. He was at Newport but little more than a year when the war (Civil) broke out, and sharing the enthusiasm and inspired by the example of the young men around him he enlisted in the Wakulla Guards, and was made a lieutenant of the company and endured the hardships and perils of those historic years, and the ranks of the Confederate army produced no soldier of finer metal, nor one who has a right to be prouder of his record. He is proud of it, and wears the Confederate button on all occasions and in all lands.

Whilst the architect of his own fortune and amassing one along lines of which his friends feel proud, he has a fine library, and has used it to advantage, and has traveled extensively, and as he is a fine conversationalist and is possessed of a splendid memory it is a rare pleasure to have him tell of his travels and discourse on current topics.

The only real thing his friends have against him is that whilst he has been vigilant in securing offices for others, he refuses to be so honored himself."

Capt. Inglis passed away after a short illness at his home in Jacksonville in 1917, he was 80 years old. He had come to this country as a boy and lived to be admired and achieve wealth and privilege. In 1906 a thorough-bred race horse named John Inglis, owned by W. H. Fizer, was also meeting with success by winning its race at Douglas Park in Louisville on September 12.

Dunnellon Phosphate Company

The Dunnellon Phosphate Company was organized in 1889, when vast amounts of hard rock phosphate were found in the vicinity of this sleepy little community. Captain John L. Inglis, who had distinguished himself on Civil War battlefields, was president of the new company. Its first shipments were made to Hamburg, Germany and London, England, in 1890, beginning a very successful and lucrative trade. By 1911, the company was operating twelve plants.

The business of the company being so great and freight rates so excessive, the founders of the company decided to handle their own shipping and, to this end, established the Port Inglis Terminal Company (P.I.T. Co.) in 1902 and made the first shipment through Port Inglis on the Dutch steamship *Themisto* on September 25. As a curious side note in history, the Themisto after taking on the load of phosphate at Port Inglis, sailed for New Orleans where she completed her load out by taking on cotton. Quite improperly and against regulations, the Public Health and Marine-Hospital Service official ordered the ship quarantined and disinfected as though she had come from a foreign port thus causing a flurry of official correspondence and complaints.

The official Federal records indicate the officials in New Orleans routinely ordered ships into quarantine so they could charge them. Dr. J.Y. Porter, State Health Officer of Florida, in a letter discussing the events he labels the events as the "Themisto affair", calls the New Orleans officials the "for revenue only crowd" and calls it a swindle and extortion!

With no government assistance, the terminal company laid thirteen and one-half miles of railroad from Rockwell (near Dunnellon) to Inglis on the Withlacoochee River, dredged the river there, and established a port on an island at the river's mouth.

The following was extracted from the first annual report of the company submitted by Superintendent of Mining Operations, G. M. Wells.

The first mining operations of the Company were begun about the first of March 1890 at a point one mile north of Dunnellon. This opening was called the "Lawtey Mine", and also Mine No. 1. Just a short while later, on the 10th of March, excavations were begun on an outcrop of phosphate rock about one quarter mile south of Mine No. 1, known as Mine No. 2.

An early mine of Dunnellon Phosphate Company. First the land was cleared of trees and brush, then the overburden of dirt was removed to get to the phosphate bearing layers of soil, and all this by hand labor. Photo courtesy of Florida State Archives Photo Collection.

Early in April, 1890, the third mine about one-eighth mile south of No. 2 was opened and work commenced at stripping. Since that time a South and North Annex to this mine have also opened and operated, both close adjoining the main excavation. This mine is our largest one, and has produced the most phosphate material and is called Mine No. 3.

On the 8ᵗʰ of June (1890), mining was commenced on a large outcrop of good material on the Hale Lands, about one mile south of Mine No. 3. This mine consists of three openings and is called the Hale Spring Mine.

On the fifth of July (1890), after careful examination of a large area north and west of the mines mentioned, a mine was opened one half mile west of the No. 1 Mine, which is called the Church Pit Mine and on the twentieth of October (1890), the uncovering of phosphate deposits, in what is known as the Z Section, was begun and this excavation is called Mine Z.

Mining work on the Withlacoochee River was commenced by hand labor, about the first of April 1890 by the use of small flat boats, and tongs and grabs, and by diving.

The total amount of shipments from all the mines has been 7,952 tons Rock Phosphate and 3,375 tons Soft Phosphate.

Twenty nine drying sheds have been erected near the various mines; five at No. 1, eight at No. 2, seven at No. 3, one at Hale Spring Mine, three at Church Pit Mine, one at the Z Mine and four at the river landing. Our drying capacity when sheds are all filled ranges from five thousand to five thousand five hundred tons.

Each of the mines has a number of small cabins and some larger barracks attached at convenient distances for the use of the laborers. The number of such houses at all the mines is about 50.

There is also erected for the use of the Mining Foremen and Engineers, a larger and better building, one room of which is used for an Office. Also a larger house for the carpenters and other mechanics not otherwise located. And a few cottages are being put up to be occupied by some of our Foremen, who have families and desire to make their homes at the mines. A small house has been built for the use of our Chemical Director, with a room attached used for preparing samples.

The first machine, worked by steam power, was erected about the first of August (1890) in the No. 2 Mine. This machine is called a "Land Trimmer" and is used to remove the superficial earth from the phosphate deposit.

This appliance consists of a long chain with scrapers attached which removes the earth to a distance of about two hundred feet and elevates the material removed about fifty feet.

A system of water works was completed in July (1890), consisting of a pumping station, water tower, and tank and about fifteen thousand feet of pipe, with hydrants at the different mines, and supply pipes for all machinery, and service pipes to some of our houses. The cost of the water works is about $3,000.

A dredging machine for river mining was purchased at Hull, England and delivered at the mines about the first of August (1890). The swift current of the river during the season of high water will always interfere with mining work as it is difficult to move even small boats against it.

The question of labor became an important one very early in our mining experience here. We have in our employ about 250 laborers and about 30 Foremen, Engineers and other mechanics.

The average price paid our laborers is one dollar a day, foremen and mechanics one and a half to two dollars. Our Chief Engineer and Surveyor are each paid $100 a month. The labor and salary account at the mines is *some $7,800 each month.* (Author's note: Typical wages in 1890 was 50 cents per day for manual labor. This would be for a man working sunup to sundown. The phosphate boom required a lot of laborers and there are reports from the period of workers abandoning their farm jobs and resulting loss of crops. The demand for workers quickly doubled wages to $1.00 per day causing men to rush to the area from all over the U.S.A. and even from Europe. For example at one period the population of the Morriston area was largely Italian.)

Photo demonstrates the intense labor requirements of the industry. Photo courtesy of Florida State Archives Photo Collection.

The S.S.O. and G.R.R. Co. (Silver Springs, Ocala and Gulf) *have laid down about four and one half miles of tracks leading to our mines at convenient points and have given us valuable assistance and provided necessary transportation facilities.*

Port Inglis

Many people believe Port Inglis was always located at the mouth of the river, at Chambers Island, but this is not correct. Originally the Dunnellon Phosphate Company considered the port to be the loading wharves and facilities located in what is today Inglis. Of course in those days the area was still called Blind Horse. A sketch of this area circa 1918 is at Appendix F.

Initially they had planned on bringing ocean going vessels up the river for loading at the Port. As early as 1879 there had been identified a need to dredge the Withlacoochee River to allow river transport of the citrus and vegetable crops to market. Much surveying and removal of snags had been performed annually since 1881. The Army Engineers had come to the realization that it would be extremely difficult to dredge the river for ocean going vessels except during the period of natural high water which was only half the year. The Federal Government continued to drag its feet on the necessary work to improve the river for traffic especially at the mouth and in 1904 the Dunnellon Phosphate Company received a permit to dredge the mouth. Accordingly, they set to accomplish what the Federal Government had failed to do. In the mean time they decided to load the phosphate onto barges which would then be taken offshore where the material was then loaded onto the ocean going vessels. It is at this point, no doubt, that someone remembered John Chambers loaded lumber onto vessels offshore in the Five Fathom Pool. The pool was relocated and buoys placed to mark the safe anchorage and shipments began.

Loading phosphate from barges onto a ship by hand in the 5 fathom pool some 5 miles west of Chambers Island. Photo from the author's collection.

There was soon a complete town on Chambers Island including custom house, coaling dock, shipyard, machine shops, commissary, hotel, school, church, houses and Capt. Inglis' Bungalow.

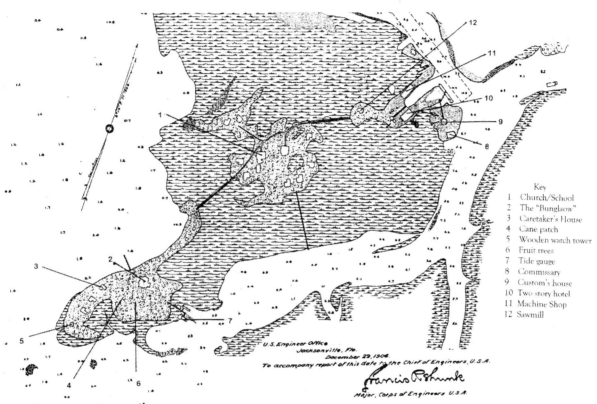

Key
1 Church/School
2 The "Bunglaow"
3 Caretaker's House
4 Cane patch
5 Wooden watch tower
6 Fruit trees
7 Tide gauge
8 Commissary
9 Custom's house
10 Two story hotel
11 Machine Shop
12 Sawmill

Original sketch if from a report by Major Francis Shrunk, U.S. Army Corps of Engineers made to the Secretary of War in 1906. Copy of report from Corps of Engineers office, Jacksonville, Florida.

The tall wooden watch tower (#5 above) located at the extreme southern tip of the island was used to keep watch over the anchorage in the 5 fathom pool. On the next page is a picture of a similar wooden watch tower. Photo courtesy of Florida State Archives Photo Collection.

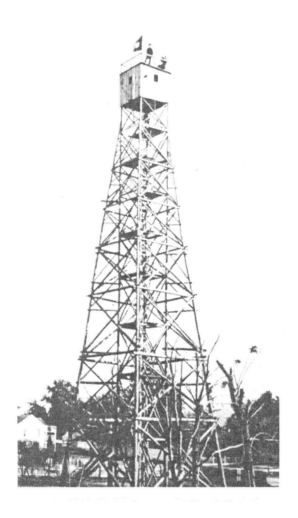

This view was taken from the Watch Tower looking north across Chambers Island. The larger building in the center is the Bungalow. Photo from the Author's collection.

The P. I. T. Co. operated as many as 43 vessels on the river at one time. As many as 60 large vessels cleared the port in a year.

Rear paddle steam tug Ralph Barker pushing P.I.T. Co. barge No. 1 down the Withlacoochee River to Chambers Island. Photo courtesy of Yankeetown School and the Knotts photo collection.

28 April 1905 Capt Inglis notified the British Consul in Jacksonville by telegram that the Spanish steamer, *Gaditno,* sank Thursday night at the entrance to the Withlacoochee River. No lives were lost as the Captain and crew swam ashore. In the May 1905 issue of *American Fertilizer* magazine we read of the account of this sinking:

A very odd and unfortunate accident occurred at Port Inglis last month. The Spanish steamship Gaditano, after completing her cargo of 3,000 tons of Dunnellon phosphate, on April 28th, cleared that evening and was anchored outside the bar buoy for the night, intending to sail the next morning for her destination, Rotterdam. At 1 A.M., through some unknown cause, the Gaditano has so far remained a mystery, being in no wise caused by local conditions. The list of lights, buoys and daymarks (sic) of the Seventh Lighthouse District shows this channel to be well marked out with buoys, beside explicit directions are given for vessels entering either from the southward or westward, and the terminal company, independent of the

Government, has gone to considerable expense to aid and facilitate ships loading at this port, but as the vessel was at anchor at the time it must have happened through some internal accident. This is the very first accident or loss to happen at this busy little port, and, therefore, the more unfortunate. Four other steamships were loading with phosphate in the harbor at the time.

By 1905, Chambers Island was being called Port Inglis and there were some 150 families, a church, school, customs house, hotel, machine shops, shipyard and commissary. A Special Post Office was established on 11 August 1905 with mail being supplied by railroad from Rockwell and thence by steamboat to the island. It would continue operating until 15 May 1916 when it closed due to the cessation of phosphate shipping as a result of the war although the numbers of ships calling at the port had greatly diminished. For example in 1912 only two vessels are known to have landed. They are the SS Cantalucia sailing from Bilboa, Spain which arrived January 22 and the SS Dora Baltea sailing from Savona via Oran which arrived December 10.

Ship sailings from or to Port Inglis during the early period are:

Nov. 10, 1902 – British ship SS Critic sailed from NY to Port Inglis
Dec. 11, 1902 – British ship SS Thomas Melville sailed from NY to Port Inglis
Sep. 17, 1903 – British steamship SS Roxby (Capt. Shields) arrived in Norfolk, Va. from Port Inglis
Mar. 29, 1904 -- SS Lyderhorn sailed from NY for Port Inglis
July 31, 1904 -- SS Mae arrived NY from Port Inglis
Dec. 25, 1904 – SS Korona sailed from NY for Port Inglis
Feb. 20, 1905 – SS Mae arrived NY from Port Inglis

Inglis

When Dunnellon Phosphate Company began building Port Inglis, the railroad terminal, Commissary and loading docks, the area was still known as Blind Horse. By 1899 the area had grown to the point that a Post Office was established to serve the 200 families in the area. The suggested name was Inglis in honor of Capt. John Inglis. After several years the community came to be called by this name and Blind Horse was lost to history.

Commissary building at Inglis circa 1920. Also housed the Post Office from 1914 to 1941. Photo from the author's collection.

By 1918, the increased traffic and the appearance of the automobile, ferries had outlived their lifespan and plans were initiated for a bridge.

Typical ferry of the period courtesy of Florida State Archives Photo Collection.

Levy County citizens were pleased with the opening of the first bridge across the Lower Withlacoochee River in 1919. This marvelous modern project was completed by the Barnes Construction Company under the budgeted cost of $3,625.00. Made of heavy oak timbers and some 148 feet in length, it was a single lane structure that served this area for many years, even after the initial single lane wagon road was replaced with a hard road.

Old timers still living in the Inglis area tell us that the superintendent of construction was well known builder and local citizen Cary Stephens. Assisting him were Mallie Kirkland, Kirby Billups and numerous others lost to history. Several important citizens from Inglis and Lebanon had petitioned the Levy County Board of County Commissioners to build a bridge to replace the outdated ferry (Blitch's Ferry) that had been built in 1885 at the eastern end of the present day Florida Power Steam Plant yard. These citizens were Frank Butler, C. J. Hodges, J. H. Anderson, C. C. Gaines, Henry Cannon and R.T. King. The original plans called for a public meeting to be held in Inglis on November 26, 1918, to consider plans for a steel bridge. Apparently the cost of such a structure and the need to serve a dirt path did not justify the expense. By June of 1919 Barnes Construction Company had been contracted to build a 124 feet wooden structure at an estimated cost of $3,500.00. Upon inspection and survey by the Federal War Department, it was decided to move the location some 100 feet necessitating a bridge of 24 additional feet in length to span the river at the new location. Barnes Construction Company agreed to this change at a nominal additional cost of $125.00. By December 2, 1919, we read in the official records that the bridge had become almost impassable by the heavy sand in its approaches and fill was required. Interestingly, this project was undertaken solely by Levy County and there is no mention of trying to get Citrus County to help pay the cost.

First bridge over the lower Withlacoochee River. Built in 1919 and located near present day four lane US 19 bridge. Photo from author's collection.

The road was one-lane dirt and the approach to the bridge required constant repair. In 1924, what is described as a "hard rock road" to Crystal River was constructed. During this period a road was considered to be "first class" when lime rock had been spread to a width of only six or eight feet over the sand trails. It could be considered an "improved" road if the two dirt ruts had been filled with lime rock!

119

By 1926 a road had been established between Inglis and Dunnellon nearby the current route of CR 40. In the Dunnellon Truth issue of 15 July 1926 we read, "The part of the Inglis-Dunnellon road in Marion County will soon be surfaced." It would not be until 1936 that the road between Dunnellon and Inglis would be improved and "surfaced", later becoming State Road 40, now County Road 40.

Road widening work by hand. Much of the road work was by convicts as shown in these two photos from the Florida State Archives photo collection.

This road would be described as "first class" although it is extremely narrow by today's standard. Photo courtesy of Florida State Archives photo collection.

Inglis Haunted ?

The Plaza 40 shopping center next to the Shell station near the intersection of US 19 and CR 40 has never been very successful. It seems anyone going into one of the shops located there has struggled. Could it be haunted?

In June of 1989, Bob Sargent of St. Petersburg had contracted to purchase the property from local developer Carroll Cason; his intention was to build a convenience store. While clearing the land at least two tombstones were discovered and evidence of a larger cemetery was exposed. According to a newspaper account (St. Petersburg Times, 19 June 1989), work was temporarily halted while "the owners and local officials try to figure out what to do". Several local citizens were contacted. Inglis Zoning Officer, Pat Adams contacted Levy County records but found no record of a cemetery "recorded" in the area. Cason's lawyer was quoted as informing the developer that he had two options: 1. Moving the graves to another site, or 2. protecting the graves and developing around it.

Local citizens provided little information as none contacted was old enough to have known of the cemetery! As with many of the old cemeteries, especially those of African American descent, this one was not recorded by the property owner when established as a cemetery, so there was no record in Levy County official records. A review of old maps of Port Inglis, however, clearly shows the black community. The Commissary was located next to the river about where the US 19 bridge currently sits. The railroad from Rockwell came along the north side of the Dunnellon road until it crossed to the south side and ran along the river next to the Commissary and on to the Barker Chemical Plant and the Dunnellon Phosphate Company barge loading chute near the old Florida Power property. The old Dunnellon road ran about where the road currently is located. On the old map, the "black quarters" are shown to be just north of the Commissary near where CR 40 intersects with US 19. The cemetery was located just at the edge of this community. For location see Appendix H.

Pictures were taken and promises given, but soon the newspapers found other stories and public interest waned….then the developers were left to their own devises and the black cemetery disappeared under the bulldozers. The only records we have are of the two tombstones last seen leaning next to an old pine in the cleared land. One reads "Sarah Putt, 1888-1927, Born a Christian, Died a Christian, Court No. 88, Dunnellon, Fla", the other smaller one reads "Ben Putt". These tombstones are now long gone as are the many graves.

Barker Chemical Company

The first recorded information about the Barker Chemical Company is found in the *American Fertilizer* magazine dated May 1904. This reference states the company was organized by the Dunnellon Phosphate Company and J. Buttgenbach & Company with capitalization costs of $500,000. They were to erect a plant at Port Inglis, probably starting in November 1904. The initial capacity was planned to be 30,000 tons per year. The plant was constructed with the option of being able to add three additional units and the engineer was Peter Gilchrist of Charlotte, North Carolina.

Barker Chemical Company warehouse. Photo courtesy of Ray Mason.

The scheme of this company was to utilize the low grade hard rock phosphate to produce an acid phosphate from 14 to 18 per cent (Note: acid phosphate is today called superphosphate). J. Buttgenbach & Co. had recently contracted to ship their own phosphate ore via Port Inglis and thus was invited to participate in the new venture.

Iron pyrites were to be imported direct from Spain on vessels chartered for the export hard rock business. Port Inglis Terminal Co. would supply steel constructed sea-going barges and tugs to transport the acid phosphate in bulk to Pensacola, Mobile, New Orleans, Galveston and all gulf and south Atlantic ports. Coal was already available as it was shipped into Port Inglis and a coaling station was maintained to supply the vessels in the phosphate trade.

Property was acquired just upriver from the then existing phosphate storage and barge loading facility on the river (current 2005 Florida Progress Energy property). Boilers, coal storage and a dryer plant were constructed along with a barge loading dock.

Bachelor quarters built for white supervisors for both Dunnellon Phosphate, Port Inglis Terminal Co. and Barker Chemical Co. workers. Photo courtesy of Ray Mason.

Untreated hard rock phosphate was first roasted (dried). The iron pyrites were roasted separately driving off sulfuric acid. The acid was applied to the phosphate and allowed to cure. This curing process took about a month and the material was kept in a large warehouse of about 500 feet by 150 feet during this time.

Large piles of slag or residue soon accumulated from this process and children used the piles for play and sought chunks of lead for use as fishing weights. In later years it would be spread on local dirt roads in an attempt to keep down the dust. Unfortunately the residue from this process contained various heavy metals including arsenic, lead and antimony.

Barker Chemical Company ran ads for its acid phosphate in *American Fertilizer* almost continuously from April 1906 until May 3, 1924, after which no further ads appeared. Its sales office was in Savannah, Georgia. Capt. Inglis' partner, Ralph Barker, was the President of the company, Robert S. Cope was Vice President and General Manager, and W. W. Mallard was the Sales Manager.

In 1925 the Florida Power Corporation purchased the portion of the property where the drying plant was located and commenced construction of a steam plant on the site which was subsequently demolished in 1993.

In February, 1995, Willard Middlestadt of Inglis had his soil tested to determine why citrus trees would not grow in his yard. To his dismay the sample showed that the soil contained elevated concentrations of arsenic, lead, and antimony. The presence of these heavy metals was soon attributed to Barker Chemical Company. In March, 1995, the Florida Department of Environmental Protection (FDEP) confirmed these heavy metals in the soil and began an investigation. In April, 1995, because of concern about exposure of residents to lead, the Levy County Public Health Unit measured the blood lead levels of about 30 adults and children living on or near the site. All test results were within the normal reference range. In February, 1996, the Florida Department of Health and Rehabilitative Services collected hair and urine samples from 25 residents of Inglis to test for arsenic. The amount of arsenic in their hair and urine was also within the normal reference range. So despite children playing on the debris piles for many years and its use as a road covering, no high levels of residue were found in any people tested.

Following a contamination assessment by the FDEP, the US Environmental Protection Agency (EPA) was requested to evaluate the site for a potential removal action. Additional sampling was completed and the EPA determined that removal of soil with elevated levels of contamination would be required to "reduce the risk of exposure to people". The removal of some 1,314 load containing approximately 29,000 tons of non-hazardous soil and 71 loads containing about 1,562 tons of hazardous material was completed in April, 1997. The tremendous cost of this removal is not mentioned in the various reports and it was thought this would complete the work. Recently

(Fall 2004) the local media has reported requests for additional testing to once again be performed.

Camp Phosphate Company Dam and Florida Power

By the late 1890s investors with Camp Phosphate Company wished to expand production while reducing labor costs with the use of electrical motors to drive conveyors and process products. In that era the only electric generators in operation were located at manufacturing plants and used only to provide power to that particular plant. For the power needed at the numerous mines in the phosphate industry, construction of numerous electric generation plants was thought cost prohibitive. The most cost effective alternative was thought to be the construction of a dam and hydroelectric plant on the Withlacoochee River and a permit was sought from the U.S. Secretary of War. In 1904, a permit was issued and work began with the purchase of land where the large reservoir would be located (now called Lake Rousseau but always known to locals as the "back water"). About this time another event would overtake this plan and it all began with ice.

In 1805 a young Boston businessman was asked by his brother "why can't the ice of New England be harvested, transported and sold to ports in the Caribbean?" Spoken simply as an off-hand remark, Frederic Tudor considered it a business opportunity or challenge and within a year he had made just such a shipment to the island of Martinique. Unfortunately much of the cargo had melted thus making the experiment unprofitable. Tudor spent time experimenting with various materials before discovering the insulation advantages of sawdust. With this discovery, he constructed ice houses throughout the tropics and created a demand for cold refreshments. In the 1820s he joined forces with a young inventor who had developed a plow-like device that scored and cut frozen ponds in New England into symmetrical blocks. By 1846 Tudor was shipping tens of thousands of tons of ice from Boston to destinations all over the world and he had become known as the "Ice King". His wealth and power would later prove disastrous for his competitors.

In 1802 John Gorrie was born on the Island of Nevis of Scotch-Irish parents but they would soon move to South Carolina where he was raised. In 1825-27 he studied medicine at the then prominent College of Physicians and Surgeons of the Western District of New York in Fairfield, New York. Initially he returned to South Carolina and practice medicine in **Abbeville** but in 1833 he moved to Apalachicola, Florida, where he practiced medicine at two hospitals and was active in the community both socially and politically. He was interested in tropical diseases and Apalachicola, like much of Florida, experienced Yellow Fever outbreaks every summer.

In that era and indeed taught in medical school, it was thought that marshy areas gave off unhealthy gases which it was believed caused various diseases. It was feared that these gases were more active at night and folk remedies incorporated the use of gauze which was hung over beds to filter the air, handkerchiefs soaked in vinegar placed over a person's nose and even garlic placed in your shoes.

Dr. Gorrie had observed in addition to Yellow Fever the outbreak of malaria during the summer months but the decline of these diseases with the change of seasons. He became convinced that swamps and marshes near populated areas should be drained and thought there might be healing power in cold air. The proof that mosquitoes spread these and other diseases would not come for several years.

His initial attempts to present cold air to his patients suffering from Yellow Fever consisted of placing bowls of ice around the hospital with a fan circulating air. Ice was expensive and didn't last long when used in this manner so Dr. Gorrie began to experiment with the making of artificial ice. Experiments of others in this field and their success were well known in the scientific community and Gorrie built his success on their work. By 1850 he had developed a mechanical device which produced ice and U. S. patent

8080 was issued to him in 1851. The notion that humans could create ice bordered on blasphemy. In a newspaper article of the day in the *New York Globe* we read of a "crank" down in Florida "that thinks he can make ice by his machine as good as God Almighty!"

Only one person had been willing to invest money in the enterprise (and he insisted on being anonymous). With his invention being ridiculed in the newspapers and the sudden death of that lone investor, other prospective investors declined to get involved. Gorrie was convinced of a smear campaign by Tudor, the Ice King. Suffering from nervous collapse and devastated by failure, Gorrie died in 1855 before his other patent application could be acted upon, a patent for what we would call today air conditioning.

Dr. John Gorrie courtesy of the Library of Congress.

By the turn of the twentieth century ice plants had proven effective and overtaken the cost advantages of ice shipments. Plants were located in most communities, even many that were quite small in size. These ice plants required electric dynamos of sufficient size to power the ice making machinery and electric lights inside the plants. Eventually people would realize that by installing a few lights and running wiring down main streets, the business sections of towns could easily be lighted thus promoting longer business days, particularly in winter with its shorter hours of sunlight. Typically these lights would burn only when the ice plants were in operation from early morning to about 10 PM. This would continue for years until it would occur to people that by running wires throughout the town, each home could be lighted. When first installed, wires were typically run through attics and through holes drilled through ceilings in the middle of some rooms. A light bulb with simple string pull for on-off switch was used.

Following the invention of the mechanical ice making machine by Dr. Gorrie in Apalachicola, ice plants began to appear in communities. One of the earliest was built in Deland in 1890 by hat manufacturer John Stetson.

In 1896, St. Petersburg Electric Light & Power Co is formed. 1897 lights go on in St. Petersburg with 30 street lights from sunset to midnight. 1910 St. Petersburg power extended to 24 hours per day. 1915 Co. was sold to investors from Baltimore and Philadelphia.1923 name changed to Pinellas Power Co. and they begin a program of consolidation, purchasing small electric plants; Bronson Mfg. Co in 1927, Inverness Power Co and Crystal River Electric Co in 1926, Dixie Power Co in 1930, Dunnellon in 1929; 1927 name changed to Florida Power Corp (although an Army Corps of Engineers report in 1915 referred to them as Florida Power).

Reportedly the investors of Camp Phosphate and Florida Power were largely the same, and we know that in August 1909, Camp Phosphate Co sold its property and dam to Florida Power (Levy Co Deed Book 4, page 597). Florida Power would then complete the hydroelectric plant in 1911. The permit required them to build and operate a lock, but the company resisted due to the expected costs. The lock was not completed until the mid 1920s just in time for the hurricane season of 1926 when it was feared the dam might fail due to extremely high water. Florida Power removed the upper portions of the lock to allow water to escape. The company would then resist repairs to place the lock back into operation until the late 1930s.

In the March 18, 1926 issue of the *Dunnellon* Truth it was announced that Florida Power planned to construct a steam plant in Inglis.

Aerial view of the Inglis Steam Plant in the late 1960s courtesy of Florida State Archives Photo Collection.

Despite the construction of this plant, Florida Power continued to deny electrical power to residents outside the larger communities, their opinion being that they could not make a profit by supplying people in rural areas. So at a time when the small electric plants were being interconnected with high voltage power lines, many people alongside those power lines would not be allowed electricity. It would not be until Congress passed the Rural Electrification Act and rural electric cooperative companies would be formed which would then provide electricity to farms and individual rural homes.

A. F. Knotts tried to get Florida Power to supply electricity to Yankeetown from the new power plant in Inglis, but they refused as Yankeetown was too small to justify the expense of running the necessary power lines. They did agree, however, to provide power if Knotts would run the lines. Knotts made a deal with Uncle Kelly Runnels for a right-of-way to run the line across his property from Inglis to Yankeetown and began construction. Runnels received free electricity for the right to cross his land. In these early days there were no electric meters. A customer would simply pay 50 cents, later $1.00 per week. Before you jump to the conclusion that this was a wonderful price, realize that extremely small amounts of electricity was being made available so the cost per unit was very high compared to today's cost. Wires would be run into an attic with holes cut into the ceilings of one or two rooms in the house with a bare bulb with pull cord hanging down to provide light. There were few electrical appliances available and they were difficult to obtain. To promote the greater consumption of power, Florida Power began selling appliances direct to their customers and even allowed payments over time.

Phosphate

Another town that appeared briefly on the scene only to soon disappear was Phosphate which was located along the railroad just south of present day Morriston. It burst into existence with the discovery of this mineral about 1891 and was awarded a post office in 1892 to serve the population of some 300 people. The U.S. Postal Service refused this name for the post office as there was already one by that name in Florida. The alternate name of Thomasville was assigned. The end of 1893 saw the end of the post office and soon the town was lost to history also.

Gladys

Even less is known of Gladys than of Phosphate. A post office was established February 26, 1900 with Samuel Y. McFarland as Postmaster. He was replaced by John W. Chapman on May 15, 1900. Exactly when the post office was disestablished is also lost. The form for requesting post offices required a sketch be provided showing the proposed location and distances from various landmarks. This information cannot be located for Gladys.

Mozo

Mozo was a turpentine community and a Post office was established 30 November 1906. On 15 May 1916 it was disestablished and mail was routed to Inglis. For location see Appendix G.

De Von

With some 175 residents working in logging and turpentine, a Post office was established on 29 March 1907 with George G. Hough as PM, Henry L. Hough took over PM on 27 November 1907. George G. Hough again named PM on 12 September 1908 and the PO was closed 15 January 1910 and mail was routed to Tidewater. For location see Appendix G.

Turpentine Industry

Turpentining, as it was called, was a thriving business in the early part of the twentieth century. The business was carried out at stills located throughout the pine tree region. The "still" might mean just the plant where the raw rosin was cooked driving off the moisture, but it could also mean collectively the plant, commissary and living quarters of the workers. Most stills were located near railroads where transportation was made easier for the heavy barrels of product.

In the old days, turpentine meant the fluid, or gum, which bleeds from a cut in a pine tree. The common meaning today of turpentine is of a clear white fluid used in medicines and paints. This product is actually spirit of turpentine and is distilled from the gum or resin. Naval Stores was the common term used for many years to describe the products: turpentine, rosin, pitch, tar and spirits of turpentine. All were used by boat builders in the days of wooden ships.

Turpentine still photo courtesy of Florida State Archives Photo Collection.

A still was a community and self contained. The still itself was of course the focal point for this is where the raw product was refined.

The commissary (the company store) was vital to both the still owner and the working hands. Business at the commissary was on credit. The hands (workers) had to make all purchases at the store. On pay day the hand was given a small amount of cash while the balance was applied to his account, which seemed always greater than his earnings. The best workers were granted more credit and were kept deeply in debt. This indebtedness tied the worker closely to the owner of the still. If the hand ran away and tried to get employment at another still (the only work he knew), he was returned. Essentially, the workers were kept in a form of bondage. It was possible to buy him out of this bondage by paying the still owner for his claimed debts. A good hand could be very expensive, and as the song goes, "he was owned by the company store".

Commissary near Inglis circa 1930. Photo courtesy Maude Price.

The hands lived in a group of shacks near the still, known as the quarters. The shacks would of course be owned by the still operator and rented to the hands. Usually a building in the quarters would be used as a church and the preacher would be one of the hands. The church would be the seat of all social activities of the quarters, just as the church would be in any community at that time.

Typical turnpentiner shack. This one located near the turpentine still at Red Level just south of Inglis in Citrus County in the early 1930s. Photo from author's collection.

These hands were termed "woods hands" as to differentiate them from the farm hands who worked in the fields or the house hands that functioned in and around the homes of the owner. A hand was born to his destiny. There was little formal education and they would be raised and taught just what there parents knew. Therefore, they followed hopelessly in the footsteps of their forefathers.

Some hands had semi-responsible jobs such as the one in charge of the still (he was called the cooker), the wagon and later the truck driver. Drivers would travel through the woods collecting the rosin and supervising the hands in the woods.

Still owners usually leased trees from land owners, paying per acres or even per tree for the right of collecting the turpentine. In a typical such contract in the author's possession, Mr. Harry R. Swartz of Tidewater, leased a small acreage to Forest Managers, Inc. of Jacksonville, Florida, and was paid by the cup hung. In 1937 he received 4 cents, in 1938, 3 ½ cents, in 1939 3 cents, in 1940 2 ½ cents and at the end of the lease in 1941 he was paid 2 cents per cup with a total number of cups at 2, 167. The trees produced more heavily the first year they were faced, thus the decrease over time.

When a new pine grove was entered for turpentining, the trees had to be prepared. Any tree over about six inches in diameter was subject to boxing (sometimes called facing). To make a face, the hand would cut two slices about eight inches long in the shape of a "V". Several such slices would be made beginning just above ground level.

Photo courtesy of Florida State Archives Photo Collection.

Two metal troughs would be nailed under the lower slices to direct the bleeding resin into containers held on the tree by a nail. Initially a hole was dug out in the tree to hold the resin, later small wooden containers were employed but they didn't hold up well in the weather. Herty pots and later aluminum containers were used.

The Herty pot above, from the author's collection, is a terricotta fluted cup. It was patented in 1903 and used throughout Florida and Georgia. Copied from a French design and made in **Daisy**, Tennessee, they were produced for only ten years, beginning in 1904. Over the years these cups have developed tone and shading that makes each one unique. Some found today may still contain bits of resin collected decades ago. They were handmade employing a mold with a small hole in the rim to hang them on the tree. A very special find is a Herty pot with a company name molded into the bottom.

Over the years, as the woods would be burned over, these pots hanging on a tree in the fire would burst. Pieces of these pots are often still found today hanging from the trunk of a long dead and burned tree.

The aluminum pots held about the same quantity of resin and were folded sheet metal, half diamond in shape when hanging on the tree. Much lighter and not breakable, they were much easier to handle and move around the woods. The one below is from the author's collection.

Most people don't recognize what this metal was used for when found today in the woods and being soft aluminum they are often flattened or crumpled into a lump and lost under the clutter of trash and leaves.

Every four to six weeks the cup would be lifted off the nail and the contents dumped into the gum barrels which were distributed through the woods. These barrels, weighing some 400 pounds, would be picked up by the wagon or truck driver and carried to the still for cooking.

Loading the heavy rosin barrels on wagon for transport to the turpentine still. Photo courtesy of Florida State Archives photo collection.

When the trees were tended and the cups dumped, a new scar or slice on the top of the face would be cut to promote the bleeding. As the new cuts were chipped into the tree, the face would increase in height, creeping up the tree at the rate of about a foot per year. On a very large tree, there would sometimes be two faces on opposite sides of the trunk.

The piney woods of Florida were often burned in those days by the cattle men who used them as range as there was no fence law until the late 1940s and it wasn't generally enforced until the 1950s. This burning seemed to draw the pitch and tar to the wood under the face and turned it into a "cat face" after the tree was cut down. Woods hands preferred to work the burned woods as it allowed them to see the many snakes and varmints.

The spirits of turpentine driven off by the heat in the cooker was condensed and poured into five gallon square tin containers or sometimes back into barrels. The by-product rosin was placed in barrels.

It was a fairly simple operation as long as the labor force was large and cheap. The company store kept the labor force together and reproduction in the quarters furnished future workers.

The bossman, always called Mister in his presence, was looked to for all necessities. He watched over his hands from cradle to grave and was judge and jury and in complete control of all aspects of life at the still.

With the advent of metal ships and the ability to obtain the turpentine raw product at paper mills and rendering plants, the turpentine business ended about the time WWII began.

Rex

Post Office established 1909 and closed 1911. It was located 737 yards "West of North" from Station B on the Standard & Hernando RR. For location see Appendix G.

Steen

Post office 10 August 1918 with Lawrence P. Knepton as PM, closed 15 January 1923, and mail routed to Tidewater. It was located in the NW ¼ of Section 1, Township 16 East and Range 17 South, just south of the Atlantic Coastline RR some 96 feet from the track. For location see Appendix G.

Tidewater

Originally called Paul, the name was changed and a Post office established 7 October 1920. It later closed 7 November 1930. This was a logging and turpentine community. For location see Appendix G.

The primary business here was the Tidewater Cypress Company owned by H. R. Swartz. The area later owned by J. T. Goethe, and sold to the state and now the Goethe State Forest, was originally owned by Swartz. His company had first logged the old growth cypress, later he leased vast acreages to other companies who collected the turpentine. There was at least one other business in Tidewater in 1925, a blacksmith by the name of A. L. West.

Yankeetown

Tom Knotts in his book, *See Yankeetown, History and Reminiscences*, tells his version of the story of this community. When writing the history of a place that includes much about one's on family, the author is tempted to embellish, even glorify the achievements while conveniently forgetting failures. In this work we will attempt to correct some things and make mention of others omitted by Knotts.

In his book he mentions *Tentative History Relative to Yankeetown and Vicinity*, an unpublished manuscript written by his uncle and founder of Yankeetown, A. F. Knotts. A copy of this work is in the possession of this author and it perhaps would be instructive to include excerpts here (comments in brackets belong to the author of the current work):

After spending many winters in other parts of Florida, hunting, fishing and trapping each year in a new locality, A. F. Knotts came to the mouth of the Withlacoochee River and spent one winter on Chambers Island, and as many others had done he stayed in a structure known as Capt. Inglis' Bungalow. The island was then owned by W. H. Boswell and was being taken care of by A. B. Easley. Mr. Easley was a man of considerable learning and well read. He was a perfect gentleman, when not drinking, which was not often. (Mr. Boswell was from Citrus County and had been involved in the phosphate business where he had come to know Capt. Inglis) *Shortly after coming to Chambers Island, Knotts was invited by Mr. Easley to go on a hunting trip with some thirteen men including John Spencer of Ocala, Mr. Galloway who was then Sheriff of Marion County, Mr. Blood also of Ocala, Mr. Thad Russell of Dunnellon, Frank Butler and his son*

Pink, living in nearby Gulf Hammock (just north of present day Inglis). *They camped and hunted for some ten days at what was known as the Leaning Tree Camp on the north side of Spring Run, east of the crossing of that creek, just north of Butler's place* (just north of present day Butler Field on the westside of Butler Road). *Knotts thus became much acquainted with the area of Gulf Hammock from Ten Mile Creek south to the river.*

After returning from this hunt, Knotts spent much time with Easley fishing and hunting along the river. Principally they hunted wildcats which were plentiful along the lower river in the vicinity that would become Yankeetown.

Learning that the river was deep, with high banks suitable for building and always free of hyacinths and that good hunting existed on both sides of the river, Knotts determined that it was the place he had been looking for to construct a hunting and fishing camp. Before Knotts left in the spring, he bargained with Alec Busbee for the purchase of 40 acres for $400 (the northeast quarter of the northeast quarter of Section 4, Township 17 East, Range 16 South).

Knotts returned the next fall and built a shanty about 20 by 30 feet in size with rough sawed lumber at the place then called Honey Bluff, a place so named because the rock bank of the river cropped out ruggedly much above high water and in this rock a swarm of bees resided and when found, contained much honey. Hugh Coleman, who then was carrying the mail from Dunnellon to Tidewater and Inglis, and the persons who lived temporarily at Honey Bluff all being from the north, Coleman called the place Yankeetown and the name stuck regardless of Knotts' efforts to make it Knotts. (A. F. Knotts had intentions of naming his community Knotts but when northerners arrived at Dunnellon and sought transportation to the new community they were directed to contact Coleman for information. Often Coleman would take passengers on his mail route and drop them at their destination which he called Yankeetown)

The name Yankeetown given by Coleman and immediately followed by the surrounding country, composed exclusively of natives, was not intended to be complimentary. Afterwards, when Knotts accepted the name and put up some signs on the road just north of Red Level, where Knotts had placed a post and attached thereto a sign, the signboard was torn off and broken into splinters and a rattlesnake hide hung on the post. It was related in New England history that once upon a time the Indians sent to the Governor of Massachusetts a rattlesnake skin filled with arrows. The Governor emptied the skin of its arrows and returned it to the Indians filled with bullets and powder. He was much braver than Knotts who simply put up another sign and continued to put them up from that time on.

It has been said that when one goes to Rome, he ought to do as the Romans do. Knotts did not follow this saying exactly, but coming to a community in Florida where it was composed exclusively of what is known as "Crackers", largely Florida Crackers, but some were from Georgia and known as Georgia Crackers, while others were from Texas, and all very much prejudiced against the people from the north. It was related by some southern speaker at one time that he was thirty years old before he knew that the word "damn Yankee" was actually two words. Knotts determined and tried to impress it upon all those that came (to Yankeetown) *that they should attend strictly to our own business and let the natives attend to their own business and have their own way, so long as they did not interfere materially with us.*

At the first registration (voting) *after I came and decided to make this my home, I registered as a Republican. There were forty-eight others registered and I was the only one without a "D" after the name. Afterwards, when I undertook to incorporate the town and believing that the word Yankeetown would attract attention from an advertising standpoint and feeling that I would not get many "Crackers" either from Florida or Georgia, to locate to the town, I decided to use the name and the Legislature was broadminded enough to incorporate the town with the name Yankeetown and designated A.F. Knotts as the first mayor.*

The corporate limits of the town was quite large, designed by myself, being four miles wide and about ten miles long, reaching from Inglis out into the

Gulf. Some of the members of the Legislature asked me why I made it so large and I told them jokingly, that I wanted it to grow. They asked me why I did not ask for an election and I told them that I had no voters and they said "why you claim to have quite a number of people" and I said "yes, but they are all Republicans and you do not allow them to vote down here!" There were many funny speeches made in the House and Senate relative to incorporating Yankeetown as "Dixieland" and electing a Republican Mayor and many jokingly claimed that they had never thought they would vote a Republican ticket! (The current city limits of Yankeetown appear to be quite large, even excessive, and indeed do extend out into the Gulf. A. F. Knotts intended this such that he could "control" this vast area. In fact the original area delineated by Knotts extended across the river into Citrus County!

Although he didn't own this land, he intended to control its development. Once this was discovered there was quite a fuss made as a city in Florida cannot extend across county boundaries. Corrections were made and Yankeetown ended up only in Levy County.)

When Kelly Runnels, formerly from Texas and a recognized leader of the local community, wished to lay out a sub-division at what is now called Crackertown, he came to Knotts and asked him to help prepare the papers and make the survey. Since then we have built a beautiful little church between the two places, for the use of both communities and hope to build a consolidated school between the two places, so that the Yankeetown and Crackertown children may grow up together and eventually forget the strife of 1861, for which none of those now living were responsible.

Tom Knotts, in Appendix U of his book, tells of some "unpleasant incidents" occurring during the settling of Yankeetown. The first story is of Willie Washington, a so called "Yankee Nigger", who drives his fancy car into Inglis one day and runs afoul of a "local" (meaning a cracker) who, influenced by moonshine, sits on the running board of the car and demands Willie get him another drink. Willie is said to have instead gone and gotten another "colored" man to help him "push" the white man from the vehicle.

Knotts tells that the affronted white men immediately got up a "mob" with loaded guns to go to Yankeetown and get Willie where they would then "hang him". Tom Knotts "conveniently" does not include the names his uncle included in the original work, nor does he investigate the incident, he simply assumes his uncle A. F. told the "whole story". At the front of the so called "mob", as confirmed by A. F. himself, was Cary Stephens, who at the time was the Justice of the Peace for the area and therefore the duly sworn officer of the law! A. F. Knotts did not "parley" with the mob as Tom Knotts suggests, but instead with the Justice of the Peace whose responsibility it was to determine if a crime had been committed, and that is what happened!

Justice of the Peace Stephens, after hearing both sides of the issue, ordered the mob to return to Inglis and disperse, which they did.

A. F. Knotts has suggested that he "built" Gary, Indiana, and many people think he was a wealthy person when he settled Yankeetown. The truth is he was a surveyor. He simply was hired to survey the area that would become the steel town of Gary. By his own admission in his tentative history, he had no intention of building a town when he came to Levy County; he simply purchased some 40 acres to build a "shanty" to hunt and fish. Knotts complained to his family in Indiana that so many people were visiting him in Florida that it was costing him too much to entertain them. Gene Knotts suggested A. F. construct a hotel or lodge and let him (Gene) come down to Florida and run it for him and charge for services, thus relieving A. F.. So in September 1923, Gene, his wife Norma, their two children, Nancy and Tom, and Norma's mother, Edith McGrath, came to Florida. What the book doesn't mention is that the only one that had wealth was Edith McGrath! If you search the records of Levy County you will discover that it was Edith that funded the settling of Yankeetown! Whenever Knotts sold land, it was the Edith who had to sign the deeds. When the water and electric works were constructed, it was Edith who owned them. Later, when she sold them to Knotts, she held a hefty mortgage on them.

Seeing an opportunity, Knotts convinced his mother-in-law, Mrs. McGrath, to acquire land which they would then sell to northerners. Knotts sought out important and influential people to help him. One, a lawyer in Orlando by the name of Eloy E. Callaway, wrote an interesting letter which is transcribed here, comments in parenthesis are this author's:

Lakeland, Fla.
October 31, 1935

Mr. Eugene Knotts,
Yankeetown, Fla.

Dear Gene:

This letter is the result of much reflection last night and today after talking to many people here in Lakeland. It is intended to be helpful to all of us, and for this reason you have my consent to show it to Judge (A.F. Knotts) *and Mrs. McGrath.*

I wish to convey the thought that nothing succeeds like success; values of almost every kind are the result of confidence, and faith in the future; that everyone avoids things which appear dead, and wants to get away from them.

I have never been associated with people whom I appreciate more than I do Judge, Mrs. McGrath and you and your family. I have never been better sold on an undertaking than I am on the building of Yankeetown. My heart and soul is in it.

I recognize that I have no right to determine the policy of development, but I would be unfaithful and unfit for the trust reposed in me, if I did not suggest things which I consider imperative.

I have the most profound admiration and respect for Judge Knotts, but I fear that he is confusing his past experiences at Gary (Indiana) *with entirely different conditions in Florida. There he was on the edge of a great growing, industrial community, supported in the outset by a hundred million dollars industrial plant. The people had to have what he had to offer, and his ability as a planner, was immediately appreciated. Here we have no such surroundings. We must create them, and can only find the way to do so, after we have found the necessary money, and that can come through publicity, and the building of an atmosphere of confidence and prosperity.*

I am pleased with the publicity which we are getting, but I think that our position is about that of a football player who fumbles the ball after the center throws it back to him. We are unquestionably fumbling the publicity which we are getting, and the reaction will be worse than if we had never had it, unless we change our atmosphere quickly.

Now, I have had not less than 25 business men here tell me that they tried to call us at Yankeetown, but were advised that the phone had been out for non payment of service charges. Nothing is more detrimental than this. Some of these men were unquestionably interested in buying property, and establishing business. That condition should be corrected, and without delay, even if you have to sacrifice a half dozen lots.

The situation there with reference to an office is almost as bad. Judge and I are both up there in a little confused office which would remind one of a country Justice of the peace office. It was all sufficient before we began to build a city. There we sit in a little room, with Judge bent over a desk and me fumbling around on a typewriter. If I were a business man or a capitalist and I should go up there with ten thousand dollars in my pocket, and intend to invest it, when I saw conditions, I would shove it back down in my pocket and leave, and that is the way they will feel.

For the present and until we can build a building, the pool table should be taken out of the room at the hotel, and that room, together with your's (sic) should be connected as an office, and the walls should be painted, suitable furniture should be installed, and a competent stenographer should be on duty to meet everyone, with a courteous statement that "Judge Knotts or Mr. Callaway will see you within a few minutes". If we want to create confidence, and thereby create values, and make some money, these things are absolutely imperative.

When one approaches the present office to go up stairs the first thing that he sees is Mrs. McGrath's car sitting there with a flat tire. By the time he gets inside the room he cannot help but wonder if the entire project is not a flat tire. Mrs. McGrath should have a new car and Judge should have one.

The time has come for us to at least have an atmosphere of confidence and prosperity if we expect to attract others to invest their money there. All the publicity in the world will amount to nothing unless this is true.

Judge has 25,000 acres (whoever gave this number to attorney Callaway overstated the facts to a huge degree). That is lots of land. There are at least 25,000 lots in 5,000 acres. Nothing in the world commands real estate confidence like building and activity. If I were in his shoes I would give away at once 1000 lots, and good ones at that, to all worthy persons who would build on them. He would still have 24,000 lots left out of his first 5000 acres, and the value that he would create in this way would run into millions. Unless he does change his ideas about the sale and development of the property it is going to be a great disappointment to all of us, and he is going to lose millions.

He should take Mrs. McGrath and go with you to some place and get him a couple of good cars at once. Trade lots for them. He should get that phone connected at once. Trade a lot for the back bill if necessary.

I do not like the way the hotel is being run. I like Lodge and his wife, but I do not like the way the hotel is operated. A newspaper man goes in there and spends a day or two. They collect every penny out of him possible. They throw away an opportunity to get a thousand dollars advertising for five or six dollars. Cities in Florida are not built that way. That hotel should be operated for one thing and one thing only, and that is to sell and build Yankeetown. You, Judge and Mrs. McGrath should make up your minds now not to try to make a dime out of that hotel for several years. Use it to entertain your prospects and to sell them on Yankeetown and get their money. George Merritte who built Corrall (sic) Gables first built two fine hotels, and he used them to sell hundreds of millions of dollars worth of real estate. If you, Judge and Mrs. McGrath will help me to create the right kind of atmosphere there, I will bring the people in there, and instead of having a village we will sell and built (sic) a great city, and all of you will make millions in doing so. It seems to me that it would be the finest kind of policy to give away a thousand lots that have virtually no present value, in order to bring in many people, and get a great building development started, so as to create tremendous value on all of his property. And since he owns the utilities, people will bring great value to him on these.

Freeman has the worse cold I ever saw. I have him full of castor oil, quinine and asperin (sic). This has delayed us here a day. We shall go South tomorrow and I am going to do my best, but for God's sake, or the sake of Science or something else in which Judge has confidence, tell him to use that great mind and vision that he has, and lets step out of the blues into the sunlight. I am writing this letter only because I may be away a week and I want all of you to begin to think about these things.

Best wishes to everybody, I am,

Sincerely,

s/ E. E. Callaway

Jail Cage

In August 1926, Yankeetown purchased from Levy County a "very large and well equipped convict cage and had it brought to Yankeetown for use as a jail" (picture on next page). The cage had been used by the County to house convicts at the site where they were working on roadways. It was a hold over from the chain gang days. The cage was mounted on four large iron wheels some 12 inches wide and could be pulled from one location to another by a mule or oxen team. The cage was about eight feet wide by 20 feet long, the sides being of crisscrossed steel straps, the ends, bottom and top of solid steel plate and a heavy door in one end. It had four tiers of three bunks at each end and a toilet seat over a hole in the bottom at the end opposite the door.

Photo courtesy of the Florida State Archives Photo Collection.

Crackertown

"Uncle" Kelly Runnels owned most of the land between Yankeetown and Inglis. He hired Knotts to survey lots which he then sold. Many of the local fishermen had been "squatting" on the various islands and land that had become Yankeetown, thus they were some of the first inhabitants of the newly opened subdivision. Being much derision between the Yankees and the locals, they naturally began calling the area Crackertown.

Peggy, Ernest and Diane Wilkerson in 1956. Photo from Author's collection.

When Yankeetown began talking of incorporating the community of Crackertown, the inhabitants were so incensed at the prospect of becoming part of Yankeetown, they petitioned Inglis for incorporation and thus Crackertown ceased to be a separate entity and was lost to history.

Yankeetown School

When A. F. Knotts came to the area in the early 1920s, there were three school districts in southern Levy County. They were Inglis, Lebanon and Fort Clinch. Schools, however, were only remaining active in the Inglis District (at Inglis and Chambers Island) and Fort Clinch (about half way on the road to Dunnellon). A great many families were dependent on fishing and were living on the islands offshore, others were living on hunting and thus lived in the Gulf Hammock. Most of the parents were illiterate and cared little about getting their children to school although a school boat was operating bringing those children to Chambers Island who wished to attend.

A bus ran to Dunnellon taking children to High School. It was a Ford Model T truck with a roof over the bed. A pine 2 x 10 running length-wise along each side and covered with oil cloth was honored by calling it a seat. The back end of the bus was not enclosed, but there was a step there to make access easier. The sides were fitted with curtains. At the beginning of the 1931-32 school year, Henry Cannon received the contract for hauling the high school students to Dunnellon. He purchased a new Chevrolet Truck and had a factory made body placed thereon.

Inglis school bus from the late 1920s or early 1930s. Photo from the author's collection.

The school at Inglis had been built during the phosphate boom and was by this time decrepit and run down. It stood on high brick piers with dilapidated steps. Hogs roamed under the building and goats slept inside. There was one usable toilet for the girls and the surrounding brush served for the boys. Most of the window panes were broken out and the door wouldn't close.

Inglis school and students in 1934-5. Left to right, front row: Kelly Runnels, Bunny Neeld, Auburn Bice. Second row: Aaron Canon, unknown boy, Lynn Neeld, Paul McMahon, unknown girl, Willadine Runnels, Peggy Robinson, Wilber Neeld, Gerald Billups, Jack Wray, Gene Runnels. Back row: Zilphia Steel, Loreen Hudson, Lorene Hawthorne, Irene Hudson, ? Starling, Babe Ruth Hawthorne, ? Munden. There were only four high school students and they were bused to Dunnellon. Photo courtesy of Dan Allen.

When several families with children had settled in Yankeetown, Knotts built a one room building to be used as a school and even furnished a teacher. Newspaper reports of the day tell us the school was about ready on 14 October 1924. His sister, Hazel Knotts, came from Gary, Indiana, to teach and she had eight pupils. The following year, Ardith Crites graduated from Indiana Normal and came to teach a somewhat larger class. Parents of children in the surrounding area where encouraged to send their children so that Levy County would help pay the expenses of the school. Eventually the County did begin to help pay expenses and by 1927 the school was so large that another building had to be constructed and the County then supplied two teachers. Later teachers would be Miss Ann Dyer, Miss Doris Delaino, Miss Way, Mr. Allen B. Walker, Mrs. Una Walker and Miss Genevieve Moore.

All this time the Inglis School continued to deteriorate and Knotts determined to get County assistance in building a large modern school. At that time each school had a Board of Trustees made up of leading men from the local area. The Yankeetown Board consisted of A. F. Knotts, Kelly Runnels (of Crackertown) and George Careman.

The first problem Knotts discovered was that there was no exact line of division established between the Inglis and Lebanon School Districts (Yankeetown School was in the Inglis School District). Knotts decided his best bet would be to get the two districts consolidated which required a vote of the people in each district. He was successful in getting the County to set a date for the election and Inglis voted in support but Lebanon held no election, therefore his consolidation efforts were smashed.

Next Knotts got a bill drawn to define the Inglis District and submitted to our representative on the Levy Board of County Commissioners, William Yearty, and he introduced and got the bill passed on 8 June 1929. Immediately Knotts called for a bond election to pay for the proposed school and there was considerable opposition. However, the bond measure passed and the bonds were validated and sent to New York Bonding Attorneys, Caldwell and Raymond, for approval. They found errors in the bill describing the Inglis District and wouldn't okay the bonds. Knotts went to Bronson to check where the error crept in, whether in the original bill or when it was printed. After he found the error was in the original bill, he realized all this work was for naught and he would have to start over again. On his way home to Yankeetown, he got the idea to stop in Lebanon and try again at getting the districts to consolidate.

This time he wisely met with Cass Robinson, the leading citizen and now patriarch of Lebanon, to see if he could get his support. After discussing the various pros and cons, Knotts discovered that Robinson's main objection to the consolidation was that Lebanon District No. 3 was much older than Inglis District No. 17, and therefore should have precedence of the newer district. Knotts wisely agreed to change his plans and agree to allow his district be consolidated into the Lebanon District, thus Inglis District was disbanded for a time. Of course the greater population was not in Lebanon and soon the school district would be renamed Inglis.

Cass Robinson on the left with good friend Henry Folks riding near Spring Run in Gulf Hammock in the 1930s. Photo courtesy of Leon Akins.

Following the second election and consolidation of school districts, bonds were approved once again, this time approval by the financiers was accomplished and Knotts began considering building plans. Initially he met with Ocala Architect Uzell, he not being very busy at the time. The depression was causing much concern and there was no hope of selling the school bonds. The option of paying the contractor directly with the bonds was not considered optimal as this would essentially mean they would be sold without competitive bidding.

By June 1933, the government announced the Public Works Administration program where they would buy the bonds so an application was made. By this time the architect, Uzell, had become quite ill, so after considerable investigation an architect in St. Petersburg, Harry L. Taylor, was selected to complete the project. Taylor and Knotts made a trip to Tallahassee with preliminary plans for the school. The state gave its approval 21 July 1934 but Taylor was not given approval to develop the final plans until November

1934. These completed plans were then sent to Washington for federal approval and were accepted 6 March 1935. Upon being returned as approved from Washington, they contained the remark by the inspecting architect, indicating that termites can get into this building by going up the front steps. Knotts and Taylor thought this was a real compliment.

Knotts' idea was that not only would the building be a school but that it could be used by the general public as well. An auditorium for public meetings was planned and also a public library manned by a paid librarian to also act as a general public relations person, to give advice and help to the local citizenry, his concern being that it was some 56 miles via Williston over poor roads to Bronson.

In the original sketch of the proposed school, we find a proposed state coastal highway on the westside of the school property. A. F. Knotts expected (according to his personal notes) that the center of Yankeetown would some day be located along this proposed route, even insisting that a minimum of 40 acres be set aside. Further, he planned that the school buildings be built several hundred yards back from the road and the front yard by used as a *"campus, making the school appear as a college"*. Long before US 19 came to be, the state had identified a need to build a road along the west coast of the state connecting Tampa with Tallahassee. Levy County Board of County Commissioners had floated a bond issue for some $3,000,000 to construct or repair several roadways. Of course when the time came to actually consider construction, they soon realized there wasn't enough money to fill in the swamp lands to actually build the coastal highway so near to the coast, thus State Road 55 which would become US 19 was built near its present location.

Also of great concern was the need for a home economics course of instruction for the girls of the area to teach them the rudiments of cooking, sewing and housekeeping. A manual training room was planned for the boys but this was never constructed.

The contract for construction was let 9 August 1935, to Ring and Topping of St. Petersburg and they started work immediately. The foundation was completed and they had started laying field stone for the walls when the government inspectors stopped them. The specifications called for field stone but added that the stone should be sound (not shale). The inspector declared the stone being used was not sound as it had holes in it and the book on testing stones indicated sound stone had not holes. Knotts called the architect but he wouldn't get involved so Knotts then called Tallahassee. They also wouldn't act so a call was made to Atlanta with the same result. A call was then made to Washington, but they simply referred Knotts back to Atlanta. The contractor was stuck and work was at a standstill with costs continuing to grow with no work being accomplished. Knotts indicated in later years that he met with the contractor and told him, "If you don't get started you're sunk. The contract calls for field stones and they are on the ground. You can't use anything else so why not disregard the inspector and go back to the job and start to work. No one has the guts to give the okay, so my bet is no one will stop you", and that is just what happened. The contractor went ahead with construction and nothing more was heard of the "holey" stones used for construction.

Construction was completed 27 April 1936 and the building accepted. The following June the contract for equipment was let and the final acceptance of the school was accomplished on 10 April 1937.

YANKEETOWN SCHOOL

Yankeetown School. Top photo taken shortly after construction completed in 1937. Photos from author's collecton.

Notice the cattle-guard in the foreground. In 1900, Florida was the only state east of the Mississippi with fewer than two people to the square mile. The great migration to the frontier had gone west, not south, thus there was no pressure to fence in the land in Florida. What doomed the open ranges of Florida were the growing metropolitan areas and the automobile. As the numbers of cars increased so also did the inevitable crashes between the two. It was common practice to fence around communities with cattle-guards built on the roads leading into town to keep the animals off city streets and out of yards. Clearly seen in the foreground in the above photo is a cattle-gap across the road leading to the front of the school. If you didn't want roaming livestock on your property you had to fence them out.

As early as 1921 pressure was building to close the open range. In Hampton Dunn's *History of Citrus County* we learn that cattlemen in that county formed the Open Range Association to fight efforts underway to force the fencing of cattle throughout the state. At that time it was reported that less than one per cent of the county was then fenced.

Over the ensuing years, pressure continued to build until 1948 when Governor Fuller Warren took office. He was determined to end the antiquated practice and promised to eliminate the open range in Florida if elected Governor. In 1949 the Florida Legislature finally acted by outlawing livestock on the highways. The open range was not immediately closed, however. Remember that enforcement of the law was the responsibility of each locally elected Sheriff. It was a slow process and took several years before the law was enforced throughout Florida. As late as 1957 I was helping my best friend and his father to move our cattle from a farm close to Dunnellon (the farm land is now in the city limits) to another farm some 6 miles north of town. On horseback we would herd the cattle through the woods usually with little difficulty as they were accustomed to the trip. Our greatest concern would be to encounter wild cattle, especially bulls that might start fights with our stock or disperse them in the woods. Some of these wild bulls were especially fearsome. After having been caught or chased by stock dogs and men on horseback with bullwhips, they occasionally would attack a man with no dogs and no whip.

Since Florida cattlemen were such a political force and able to prevent a law requiring the fencing in of livestock, the result was that cattle roamed the highways with more rights than a human driving an automobile, like the animals in the picture above on what is today John F. Kennedy Boulevard in Tampa.

The Inglis area became quite involved in this heated battle to fence livestock. The late Dewey D. Allen, long time Mayor of Inglis, was elected a second time to the Florida Legislature in 1948. His opponent, D. P. McKenzie was supported by the local cattlemen but he lost by one vote. No recount was requested so Allen prepared to take office. Reportedly the cattlemen went to Allen and demanded he fight Governor Warren's cow bill. Allen was quoted as saying he wasn't much of a politician and told them "I'm not going to do one thing for you." The cattlemen then told him the next election they would get rid of him. Allen was assigned to the livestock committee and after reflection; he offered an amendment to the cattle bill to postpone the effective date to July 1 of the following year to allow cattlemen time to build fences. When Allen ran for re-election the cattlemen remembered and ganged up and "really threw me out", as he tells it. Later the cattlemen came back to Allen and told him when the cattle were fenced in pastures and after culling out the non-producers they were having less trouble and making more money. "We feel we made a mistake," they said. If you'll run again, we'll support you. But Allen tells that legislators were receiving $360 a year for a 60 day session and he couldn't afford to run for that little money!

With the opening of the Yankeetown School for the 1938 school year, the other schools in the district were closed. Children from Inglis, Chambers and other islands were then sent by bus and boat to the new school. The school boat, the "Pumpkin Seed" would pick up children from Chambers and other islands, delivering them to a landing at the Izaak Walton Lodge where they would then catch a bus.

This boat is from the same period and similar to the *Pumpkin Seed*. Photo courtesy of Levy County Genealogy and History Society.

The next controversy involving the school would occur in 1949 when talk began of building a large high school in Bronson and busing all students to that central location. The Yankeetown School would then become only a elementary and middle grade school once again.

Oil in Levy County?

Excitement abounded in 1938 when the Houston Oil Company came to Levy County in search of gas and oil. When nothing was found, business people and land owners hoped they just hadn't done a good job. In June of 1940, H.R. Swartz of Tidewater, B.S. Stutts of Dunnellon, and Joe Savory of Inverness formed a partnership with M.G. Eitelman as their agent. They planned to encourage the search for oil, gas and mineral wealth in lands in Levy, Citrus, Sumpter and the west ½ of Marion Counties, but as we know today, the oil and gas is off the Gulf Coast.

Early drilling rig courtesy of Florida State Archives photo collection.

Appendix A

Andrew E. Hodges and Others V. the State
(no number in the original)

Supreme Court of Texas

1857, Decided

Prior History: Appeal from Guadalupe. Tried below before the Hon. Thomas H. DuVal.

Wednesday, 14th May, 1856. The State v. Hodges. No. 262. Comes the District Attorney on behalf of the State, and the defendant being three times solemnly called to come into Court and answer an indictment exhibited against him by the grand jury of Guadalupe county for assault with intent to kill, came not but made default; and the securities of the said Andrew E. Hodges, to wit: Miles Elkins, John C. Sheffield, W. H. C. Johnson, A. E. Knowles, Joseph Hawkins, P. R. Oliver, Y. P. Outlaw, being also three times solemnly called to come into court and bring with them the body of said Hodges, came not, but also made default. It is therefore considered that the bond of said parties, of date the 3rd day of January 1856, for the sum of twenty-five hundred dollars, be forfeited to the State, and that scire facias issue thereon to said parties returnable to next Term of said Court.

Here followed a bond of said Hodges and his said sureties, in the sum of $ 2,000, dated January 3rd, 1856, conditioned, that whereas said A. E. Hodges has been arrested and tried before W. B. Whitlock, an acting Justice of the Peace in and for the county of Guadalupe, on a charge of an assault with an intent to kill one John Christopher; and whereas said Hodges has been this day held to bail on said charge in the sum of two thousand five hundred dollars; now if the said Hodges shall make his personal appearance on the first day of the next Term of the district Court and no depart the same without leave, then this bond will be void, otherwise it will remain in full force and virtue. (signed and sealed, and approved by the Sheriff of Guadalupe county.)

Scire facias to each of the parties, reciting that whereas at the Spring Term, 1856, of the District Court of Guadalupe county, a judgment nisi was rendered upon a forfeited bond for the sum of twenty-five hundred dollars, against Andrew E. Hodges and his sureties, naming them, because the said Hodges failed to appear at the said Term of the District Court and answer to the charge of an indictment exhibited against him for an assault with intent to kill on John Christopher on the 25th day of December, 1855. It them commanded the Sheriff to summon said sureties, by name, to show cause at the next Term os said court, to be holden, & c., why said judgment should not be made final.

At Fall Term, 1856, defendants demurred generally to the judgment nisi and scire facias; and alleged in general terms that the recognizance was void, of which in one paragraph they prayed the judgment of the Court; and in another they declared their readiness to prove it. They also moved in general terms to dismiss the judgment nisi. Entry of motion to quash the bond overruled, and leave to defendants to amend their answer.

Amended answer alleging that said bond or recognizance is void for the following reasons: That it was not taken or approved by the proper officer; that the penal sum mentioned in said bond was not fixed by the Justice of the Peace; that it does not show defendant was charged with an indictable offence, but does show that he was charged with the commission of an act not indictable; that it does not show in what county said act charged was committed; that is does not show, in the condition thereof, at what District Court or in what county, defendant was to make his appearance.

And for further cause why said judgment nisi should not be made final, these defendants say that said Hodges was not committed to the jail of the county by any Justice of the Peace.

Here followed a motion by the District Attorney, for leave to amend the scire facias by making a copy of the bond a part thereof, and by striking out the word "indictment". No action appears to have been taken on this motion.

The cause being called for trial, the Court, after hearing the argument of counsel and inspecting the record, made the judgment nisi final. It is therefore considered, &c. rendering judgment for $ 2500. Motion for new trial, on same grounds already stated; overruled. This is a complete statement of all that appeared in the transcript.

Disposition: Reversed and reformed.

Headnotes: To sustain a recognizance (in the absence of a commitment and transcript of the proceedings in the Justice's Court,) taken and approved by the Sheriff (under Art. 1706, Hart. Dig.) it is not necessary that it should recite that the defendant had been committed to jail by the Justice of the Peace; it is sufficient if it recite that he has been tried by the Justice of the Peace, and held to bail.

Where bond taken and approved by the Sheriff (under Art. 1706, Hart. Dig.) recites that the defendant was tried by a Justice of the Peace and held to bail in a certain amount, it sufficiently appears that the defendant was committed to jail or to the custody of the Sheriff until he should find bail, in the amount fixed by the Justice.

Where it appears from a recognizance or bond, that the defendant was held to bail by a Justice of the Peace of a county named, to appear at the next Term of the District Court, it must be intended that it was the District Court of the same county, and the recital is sufficient.

If in point of fact, the accused had not been committed, or the offence was cognizable in another county, these matters might have been pleaded in avoidance of the recognizance.

A recognizance or bond to appear and answer a charge of "assault with intent to kill," is good, because, under such a charge the defendant could be convicted of an assault, if not also of the intent to murder.

Where the obligatory part of a bond to appear and answer, taken and approved by a Sheriff (under Art. 1706, Hart. Dig.) was in the sum of $ 2,000, and the condition recited that the accused was held to bail in the sum of $ 2,500, it was held that the only effect was to reduce the judgment, which had been entered for $ 2,500 to $ 2,000.

Counsel: Hancock & West, for appellant.
I. The recognizance should have been approved by the Justice of the Peace. Art. 1706, Hart. Dig. Shows when the Sheriff has power to approve; it is only after the party has been committed to jail. Art. 1709 is conclusive on this part.

II. The amount of the recognizance was never fixed by the Justice of the Peace; this was not necessary where the Justice previously acted, but was acquired by the statute, when the Sheriff or any other officer took the recognizance. (Art 1706, Hart. Dig.)

III. There is no indictable offence charged in the recognizance. The words "kill and murder" should have been used. (Hart. Dig. Art. 372; Id. Art. 508; Dailey v. The State, 4 Tex. R. 417; State v. Cotton, 6 Ed. 425.)

IV. The recognizance is void because it does not show in what county the offence was committed, nor where the defendant is to appear to answer the charge. (Hart. Digi. Art. 1704).

V. The condition is not drawn in conformity with the statute, and is therefore a nullity; it is defective in this, 1st, that it does not say, as required by the statute, in what county he is to appear; 2nd, it does not require him to "appear and answer the charge" as required by the statute, but simply that he shall make his "personal appearance." (Hart. Dig Art. 1704). Where the statute prescribes the form of a bond, it should be pursued. (Hammons v. The State, 8 Tex. R. 272; Lawton V. The State, 5 Id. 270).

Attorney-General, for appellee:
I. It may be granted that, as the statute designates a certain offence as an assault with intent to murder, this form of words would be absolutely required to express that degree of crime. But an indictment for an assault with intent to kill would sustain a verdict for aggravated assault or assault and battery. But supposing the allegation would be only sufficient to sustain a charge for simple assault, still this is an indictable offence and the bond is good. In Alabama it was ruled that under an indictment which charged an assault with intent to kill and murder, a verdict of assault with intent to kill is not a conviction for the principal charge, but is good as a conviction for assault and batter. (State v. Burns, 8 Ala. R. 313).

II. It is further objected that the bond was not taken and approved by the proper officer. It recites that the defendant had been held to bail by a Justice of the Peace of Guadalupe county and the bond is approved by the Sheriff. The exception narrows itself down to this—that the bond should have recited the commitment of the accused in default of bail. This is a mere verbal criticism. The recitation is substantially the same as if this had been expressed.

III. As to the amount being fixed by the Justice, this objection is contradicted by the bond, which expressly recites that after examination the accused had been held to bail in the specified amount. There is a discrepancy between the amount first stated in the obligation and the amount afterwards recited in the condition. This is unimportant except that it may reduce the judgment to the amount first set out.

IV. It is objected that the bond does not show in what county the offence was committed, and that the bond does not specify before what Court the defendant is bound to appear. An inspection of the bond, and any fair construction of its terms will, it seems to me, be sufficient to overcome these objections.

Upon the whole, unless a rule as rigid as could be demanded upon the final trial of a capital cause, is applied to these proceedings, they must be held sufficient.

Judges: Wheeler, J.

Opinion by: Wheeler

Opinion: The recognizance appears to have been taken under Article 1706 of the Digest. It does not recite that the principal recognizor had been committed to jail; nor, it is conceived, was it necessary that it should so recite.
It sufficiently appears that the Justice in admitting the accused to bail, did fix the amount of the recognizance. Having been committed to jail or to the custody of the Sheriff until he should find bail, that Officer was authorized to take the recognizance.

The accused being held to bail by a Justice of the county of Guadalupe, to appear at the next Term of the District Court, it must be intended that it was the District Court of the same county. If the offence had been cognizable in any other county, the Justice must have sent the accused before an officer of the county having cognizance of the offence, for examination and trial, instead of holding him to bail, as he did. (Hrt. Dig. Art. 1704).

If, in point of fact, the accused had not been committed, or the offence was cognizable in another county, these matters might have been pleaded in avoidance of the recognizance.

It cannot be said that the recognizance does not require the accused to answer to an indictable offence. An "assault with intent to kill" is an offence, for which the accused might be convicted of the assault, if not also of the intent to murder. We think the recognizance legally sufficient. But it bound the defendants in the sum of two thousand dollars only; and they were not liable upon it beyond that sum. The judgment is therefore erroneous and must be reversed, and the proper judgment be rendered.

Reversed and reformed.

Appendix B

Supreme Court of Texas

The State v. A. E. Hodges

October 1860 Decided

Prior History: Appeal from Guadalupe. Tried below before Hon. A. W. Terrell, one of the district judges.

The petition of the appellant alleged the forfeiture of the bail-bond of the appellee, Hodges and his sureties, for the amount thereof, to wit, $ 2,500, and a judgment final of the district court rendered thereon; that these appellees then appealed to the supreme court; that the district clerk made a mistake in the transcript of the record for the supreme court, whereby the bond therein appeared to be in the sum of $ 2,000 instead of $ 2,500, as the original is in fact written; that the judgment of the district court was by the supreme court reversed and reformed, rendering its judgment in favor of the state against these appellees (then appellants) for the sum of $ 2,000. The petition prayed for a correction of the mistake, by rendering judgment against principal and sureties for the sum of $500.

The defendants demurred to the petition; demurrer sustained and cause dismissed.

Disposition: Affirmed

Headnotes: The existence of a clerical error in the transcript of the record whereon this court has rendered its judgment, decisive of the whole case, will not afford ground to one of the parties to go h=behind that judgment, and, by alleging in a new action the error, maintain a suit for a cause depending upon such omission.

All errors in the record should be corrected before this court makes its decree.

Counsel: Geo. Flournoy, Attorney General, for the state. John Ireland, for the appellees.

Judges: J. Bell

Opinion by: Bell

Opinion: We are of opinion that the court below did not err in sustaining the demurrer to the petition.

The appeal in the case of Hodges and others against the State, reported in 20 Tex. Page 493, brought that whole case into this court, and this court adjudicated all the matters presented by the record then before it. The judgment of the district court was, in point of fact, reversed by this court, and the judgment which was rendered by this court is the only judgment in that case.

There is no power to go behind that judgment because there was a clerical error in the transcript of the record. All errors in the record should be corrected before this court makes its decree. The judgment of the court below is Affirmed.

Appendix C

1896 Supreme Court Appeal, Florida

William H. Anderson, As Administrator, Etc., of A. E. Hodges, deceased, Plaintiff in Error, Vs. E. W. Agnew & Co., Defendants in Error

Supreme Court of Florida

38 Fla 30; 20 So. 766; 1896 Fla
June 1896

Prior History:

Writ of error to the Circuit Court for Levy County

Statement: The defendants in error, who were plaintiffs below, on May 18th, 1881, brought their action in trover against A. E. Hodges in his lifetime. The declaration alleged the conversion to his own use by said Hodges of 499 sticks of cedar timber belonging to the plaintiffs. To this decaration the defendant Hodges plead not guilty. Some other pleas were filed by the original defendant, but there being no contention that they are sustained by the evidence in the case, there is no need of further mention of them. No further action seems to have been taken in the case until October 27th, 1886, when the plaintiffs filed in the clerk's office a written suggestion of the death of the defendant, and in such suggestion stated that Charles B. Rogers was duly qualified as an executor of the deceased, and prayed that he be made a party defendant in the case. On the 20th of said month a notice had been issued in the case directed to Charles B. Rogers, as executor of the defendant, requiring him to appear on the first Monday in November then next and to show cause why he should not be made a party defendant in said cause, and that in default of such appearance judgment would be rendered against him by default. A copy of this notice as well as a copy of the original summons in the case and also of the written suggestion above referred to, were served upon said Rogers as such executor on October 21st, 1886, in Duval County, Florida, by the sheriff of such last named county. The record contains a recitation by the clerk that the defendant, by his attorney (without naming him), entered his appearance in the case on the first day of

November, 1886. No further proceedings were then had until April 26th, 1888, when the plaintiffs filed in the clerk's office a certified copy of the order of the County Judge of Levy County, Florida, showing that the said C. B. Rogers, executor of the last will and testament of A. E. Hodges, deceased, had been "relieved from further duties as such executor," and that the defendant, William H. Anderson, had been appointed on April 7th, 1888, "administrator de bonis non cum testamento annexo of the last will and testament of said A. E. Hodges, deceased." At the same time of filing said certified copy of said order the plaintiffs filed their written suggestion of the removal of Rogers as executor, and of the appointment and qualification of the defendant Anderson as administrator cum testamento annexo, and prayed that said Anderson as administratior be made a party defendant, and that summons ad respondendum be issued to him. Notice and summons were issued and served, and an order was made by the court May 7th, 1888, making said Anderson, as such administrator, a party to the suit. The defendant Anderson, as administrator de bonis non, etc., on June 3rd, 1888, filed a plea, in substance , that on the 9th day of January, 1886, Charles B. Rogers was the duly qualified and acting executor of the estate of the said Andrew E. Hodges, deceased, under the will of the said Hodges, and that on that day the said Rogers, as said executor, by an advertisement published once a week for eight consecutive weeks in the Florida State Journal, a newspaper printed in the county of Levy and State of Florida, the first publication of said advertisement being on the said 9th day of January, 1886, gave notice to all persons having claims or demands of any kind against the said Andrew E. Hodges, deceased, to present the same within the time prescribed by law, or that said notice would be pleaded in bar of their recovery; and that the claim or demand sued for in plaintiff's declaration was not presented or exhibited to the said Charles B. Rogers, as said executor, or to any other representative of said estate within two years after said publication.

Issue having been joined upon the please, the case was on November 29th, 1889, by consent referred to John G. Reardon, Esq., a practicing attorney of the court, as referee therein for trial. On June 9th, 1890, the referee filed an order dated June 7th, 1890, reciting that the case "coming before me as referee upon the defendant's plea of the statute of non claim filed therein, and argument having been submitted by both parties thereto, and having duly considered the same, it is ordered and adjudged that the said plea be and the same is hereby overruled and not allowed." On June 24th, 1890, the case came on for trial before the referee, who found for the plaintiffs and assessed damages at $ 1,362.27, and $ 1,216.11 interest, total $ 2,578.38, besides costs. A motion for new trial being denied, the defendant takes writ of error.

The errors assigned and argued are the overruling the plea of the statute of non claim and in rendering judgment for the plaintiffs upon the evidence in the case.

Other facts are stated in the opinion of the court.

Headnotes: (Judge call, of the Fourth Judicial Circuit, sat in the place of Mr. Justice Taylor, who was disqualified).

1. Where the entry of an appearance by the defendant is relied upon in this court as curing defects in the service of process, such entry of appearance is a matter that should appear affirmatively and distinctly from the record. A mere recitation by the clerk in a transcript of a record upon a writ of error made before the adoption of Special Rule No. 3 of the Circuit Courts (September 16th, 1895), that a defendant entered an appearance by some unnamed attorney, is not sufficient to show that defendant actually appeared in the case.

2. A suggestion of the death of the defendant stating the name of his duly qualified executor, and praying that such executor be made a party defendant in the case in accordance with the rule of court and statute governing such proceedings, when duly filed within the time limited by aw for the presentation of claims, is equivalent to and dispenses with the actual presentation of the claim upon which the suit is brought.

3. In an action of trover the plea of not guilty raise no issue as to the plaintiff's property in the goods alleged to have been taken and converted by the defendant. Such plea only operates as a denial that the defendant committed the wrong alleged, i. e. , that he took and converted the goods to his own use.

4. Under a plea of not guilty, the general issue in trover, the defendant can not prove the property or right of possession of the chattels in question to be in some other person than the plaintiff.

5. The purpose in an action of trover of proving a demand and refusal is to show a conversion of the property; and it is wholly unnecessary to prove a demand where the conversion is otherwise shown.

Counsel: Thos. F. King, for Plaintiff in Error.

Geo. H. Badger for Defendants in Error.

Opinion by: J. Liddon

In the argument upon the assignment of errors predicated upon the overruling of the plea of the statute of non claim no question is raised as to the manner in which the ruling was made. Without reference to the procedure, the plaintiff in error contends that upon the record and the evidence in the case the judgment upon this plea should have been for the defendant. We consider the case as presented. Although the plea in question was overruled before the trial was had upon the other please, the defendant offered, without objection, his evidence to sustain such plea. Considering the proof of publication of the notice to all persons having claims against the estate of the deceased to have been duly made as alleged in the plea, the question arises whether the proceedings taken in the case against Rogers, as executor, within the time limited by the statute for the presentment of claims was equivalent to a presentation of the demand sued upon, or dispensed with the necessity of such presentation. In considering such question the transcript being filed before the adoption of special rule No. 3 of Circuit Courts adopted Sept. 16th, 1895, we do not consider as of any validity the recital of the clerk that the defendant appeared by his attorney in the case. It is well settled by many decisions of this court that a voluntary entry by a party defendant or his authorized attorney of a general appearance in a cause, or the doing of any act fully equivalent to such entry of a general appearance, cures all defects in the service of the writ, and is legally conclusive that such party had notice of the demand sued upon, and gives the court jurisdiction of his person. But such entry of appearance, or its equivalent act, is a matter that should appear affirmatively and distinctly from the record. Where the defendant has not been legally served with process, or has filed no plea, or taken any other step to defend the suit, a mere recitation by a clerk in a transcript of record upon a writ oerror that he entered an appearance by some unnamed attorney, is not sufficient to show that he actually appeared in the case. Barker vs. Shepard, 42 Miss. 277, and other Mississippi cased cited in test, pages 282 et seq.; Crary vs Barber, 1

Colo. 172; Kimbal vs. Merrick, 20 Ark. 12. Therefore, if the effect of the statute of non claim is avoided by the proceedings taken against Rogers, as executor, it must either appear that a legal notice or writ issued against him in the case, and was served upon him, or that such issuing and service were unnecessary. The suggestion of the death of the defendant, filed, to make said Rogers, as executor, a party was in strict compliance with Circuit Court Common law Rule 36, and with the statute then in force (sec. 75, p. 830 McClellan's Digest; sec. 45, chap. 1096 laws of Florida, acts of 1861). The plaintiff did all that was incumbent upon him and the proper writ or notice should have been issued by the clerk. We do not think it necessary to determine whether a notice in due and legal form was taken by the plaintiffs to revive the suit against Rogers, as executor for the deceased defendant being taken within the time limited by law for the presentation of claims is equivalent to and dispenses with an actual presentation of the claim. In Ellison vs. Allen, 8 Fla. 206, the defendant died after service of process. The statute (act of 1838, sec. 3, p. 332 Thompson's Digest) then in force required that upon the death of a party defendant to a suit the plaintiff might sue out a scire facias requiring the executor or administrator of the defendant to appear and answer the cause. Said scire facias was to be served in the same manner pointed out by statute for the service of other process. After the death of the defendant, but before the expiration of the time limited by statute for the presentation of claims to the administrator, the plaintiff asked for and obtained an order for a scire facias to make such administrator a party defendant in the suit. The administrator seems to have lived, and administration to have been granted, in a county other than that where the suit was pending. No scire facias was issued upon the order. The court held that the obtaining of the order for the scire facias was equivalent to and dispensed with the actual presentation of the claim. In the conclusions, which are unnecessary to be repeated here. The suggestion filed in the case under consideration, and the notice issued in pursuance thereof, were under the provisions of the a later statute, and were substitutes for the former proceedings by scire facias. They were substantially the same character of proceedings; the difference between them being more nominal than real. It was as much the duty of the clerk to issue the proper notice under the suggestion filed by the plaintiffs as it was his duty under the old law to issue the scire facias upon the order of the court therefore. The rule applied in Ellison vs. Allen, supra, is properly applicable to this case. In Bush vs. Adams, 22 Fla. 177, this court held that the facts of the case did not come within the principle of Ellison vs. Allen, but in the opinion it is stated to be a duty to apply the principle to cases falling within it, although the doctrine announced is as liberal as the terms and policy of the statute will sustain. The reasons are stronger in this case than in Ellison vs. Allen why the proceedings taken to make the executor, Rogers, a party should be held equivalent to a presentation of the claim, or sufficient to dispense with such presentation. In that case no scire facias issued at all, and there is nothing to show that the administrator had within the time limited by the statute of non claim any knowledge or notice whatever of the suit. In this case the notice actually issued as provided by statute, and while these may perhaps not have been in perfect legal form, and legal service of it may not have been made, there was a notice actually issued in fact, and notice and knowledge of the suit as a matter of fact brought home to the executor.

It is also contended that upon the evidence submitted upon the plea of not guilty the judgment should have been for the defendant. Among other matters wherein it is claimed that the plaintiffs failed to sustain their case it is argued that the plaintiffs did not show a sufficient title to the property which they charged the defendant with converting to his own use, and that the title to the land from which the sticks of cedar in controversy were taken was not in the name of the plaintiff's firm, but stood in the name of one of the plaintiffs individually, and another person. Unfortunately for this contention there is no plea in the case which presents any issue as to plaintiffs' title. The plea of not guilty raises no issue as to the plaintiffs' property in the goods alleged to have been taken and converted by the defendant. It only operates as a denial that the defendant committed the wrong alleged, i.e., that he took and converted the goods to his own use. Circuit Court Common Law Rule 75; Stewart vs. Mills, 18 Fla. 57. Under the plea of not guilty, the general issue in trover, the defendant can not prove the property or right of possession of the chattels in question to be in some other than the plaintiff. Robinson vs. Hartridge, 13 Fla. 501, text 508 et seq.

It is contended that the findings of the referee were not supported by the testimony, because such testimony, fails to show a taking and conversion of the property by A. E. Hodges. It would serve no useful purpose to sumup or analyze the testimony, and we do not do so. We deem it sufficient to say that while it was not so full, complete and satisfactory as it might have been, yet it was sufficient to authorize the referee to find for the plaintiff.

It is also contended that the plaintiffs should not have maintained their suit because they made no proof of a demand before suit was brought. The record does show proof of demand made upon Joel Hodges, the agent of the deceased defendant A. E. Hodges. It was not necessary, however, to have proven such demand. The proof of the conversion being complete, no proof of demand before suit was necessary. The purpose in an action of trover of proving a demand and refusal is to show a conversion of the property, an it is wholly unnecessary to prove a demand where the conversion is otherwise shown. Robinson vs. Hartridge, 13 Fla. 501, text 515; 26 Am. & Eng. Ency. Of Law, 728.

The judgment of the Circuit Court is affirmed.

Appendix D

Will of Dr. Andrew E. Hodges. Levy County Will Book 1, pages 5-6, transcribed by the author.

I Andrew E. Hodges of the County of Levy and State of Florida mindful of the uncertainties of human life do make publish and declare this to be my last will and testament in manner following:

1st. After the payment of my just debts and funeral expenses I give devise and bequeath to my four sons Culpepper Hodges now about sixteen years old, Randolph Hodges now about fourteen years old, Jules Hodges now about twelve years old and Ruff Hodges now about ten years old all of my estates both real and personal and in case any one or more of my said four sons above named should die before reaching the age of twenty one years then and in that case it is my will and I give devise and bequeath to the survivors of my said four sons whose names are above and before written all of my estates both real and personal.

2nd. I hereby nominate and appoint my friend Charles B. Rogers of the City of Cedar Key, County of Levy and State of Florida the executor of this my last will and testament and the guardian of such of my said four sons whose names are above written as may be under the age of twenty one years at the time of my death and I do hereby authorise (sic) and empower the said Charles B. Rogers the executor of this my last will and testament to compound, compromise and settle any claim or demand which may be against or in favor of my said estates on such terms as he may think best for the interest of my said estates.

On witness whereof I have hereunto set my hand and seal as and for my last will and testament.

s/ Andrew E. Hodges

Signed published and declared by the said Andrew E. Hodges to be his last will and testament in the presence of us who have signed our names at his request as witnesses in his presence and in the presence of each other.

s/   E. F. Oneill   J. E. Richards   F. H. Patrick

Appendix E

The Preemption Act of 1841

In 1841, Congress enacted a general preemption statute applicable to all surveyed public lands, offered and unoffered. The Preemption Act of 1841 permitted the head of a family, a widow, or a single man over 21 years of age with a one-time opportunity to preempt up to 160 acres of land within the public domain. The law required that the preemptor be a United States citizen or have filed a declaration of intent to become a citizen. In addition, a preemptor could not own more than 320 acres in any state or territory. The Preemption Act was amended in 1862 to include unsurveyed lands.

The statutory preemption price was $ 1.25 per acre. But, in the case of land within the alternating sections of the land granted by the federal government to the railroad companies, a claimant was required to pay the higher preemption price of $ 2.50 per acre. Up to 160 acres could be preempted in these alternating sections.

If a preemptor settled on unoffered or unsurveyed lands, he was required to file an intention to preempt within three months of settlement. He was required to prove up and pay the preemption price no later than 33 months after the date of settlement, but could prove up as early as 6 months from the date of settlement if desired. If a claimant settled on previously offered lands, he had 30 days from the time of settlement to obtain a preemption certificate from the land office. He had only 12 months from the date of his preemption certificate to prove up and pay the preemption price, but as with unoffered lands, he could prove up as early as 6 months from the date of settlement if desired.

In connection with proving up his claim, a preemptor was required to attest, and to have two witnesses who could also attest, that he met the requirements of the Preemption Act and that the preemption claim had been his primary residence for the applicable time period.

Appendix F

The Homestead Act of 1862

The Homestead Act of 1862 provided an eligible person with up to 160 acres in return for five years residency and $ 18 in fees (an initial filing fee of $ 14 with an additional $ 4 in fees at final proof). The Homestead Act provided that any individual who was the head of a family or at least 21 years old (or who had performed military service for the United States) could homestead up to 160 acres. A homesteader was required to settle his claim within six months of filing with the land office and to prove up by no later than seven years from the filing date.

Like preemption, an individual was entitled under the law to make final proof on one homestead claim. Despite the prohibitions against more than one homestead per individual, numerous instances of fraud are known to have occurred, with individuals entering multiple preemption and homestead claims under different names or in different states.

Although the Homestead Act applied to all lands subject to preemption, the extension of preemption to unserveyed public lands occurred after enactment of the Homestead Act. Consequently, homesteads could only be claimed on surveyed public lands. There were several limitations on the public land available for homesteading. The federal government gave substantial tracts of public domain land to the railroad corporations for the construction of railroad lines and to the individual states and territories for public schools and other purposes. In the mid-1800s, there was also a vast reserve of land not yet ceded by various Indian tribes. This land was not available for preemption or homesteading prior to cession.

The Homestead Act did not supersede the Preemption Act, and as long as a homesteader could fulfill the applicable residency requirements when proving up each claim, an individual could take out both a preemption and a homestead claim.

Alternate sections within the railroad land grants remained in the public domain and were subject to preemption and homestead; however, homesteaders were originally limited to a maximum of 80 acres within these alternating sections. Any soldier who had served more than 90 days was allowed to homestead up to 160 acres and to deduct up to four years served from the residency requirement.

Most settlers acquiring land under the federal land laws of preemption and homestead selected claims outside the limits of the railroad grants, and while they acquired "cheap" or "free" land by doing so, they often limited their chances for success by settling farther away from transportation and civilization. Homesteaded land was often referred to as "free" land since the only cash outlay was payment of the required filing fees.

Appendix G

PHOENIX
JERICHO
PHOSPHATE
EVE
RALEIGH
BARCO
CAMP SPUR
MEREDITH
ALBION
JUDSON
PLEASANT GROVE
TIDEWATER
STEEN
DE VON
WITHLACOOCHEE RIVER
BLACK DIRT
DAM
REX
MOZO
LEBANON
LEBANON STATION
INGLIS
PORT INGLIS
Hodges (1)
Hodges (2)
GUNTOWN
LENNON
ECHO
FORT JENNINGS
LEVYVILLE
GORE
DOUBLE SINK
WACASSASA
JOPPA
JANNEY
DANIEL
ROCKY HAMMOCK
ELLZEY
WYLLY
VISTA
SUWANNEE RIVER
ATSENA OTIE

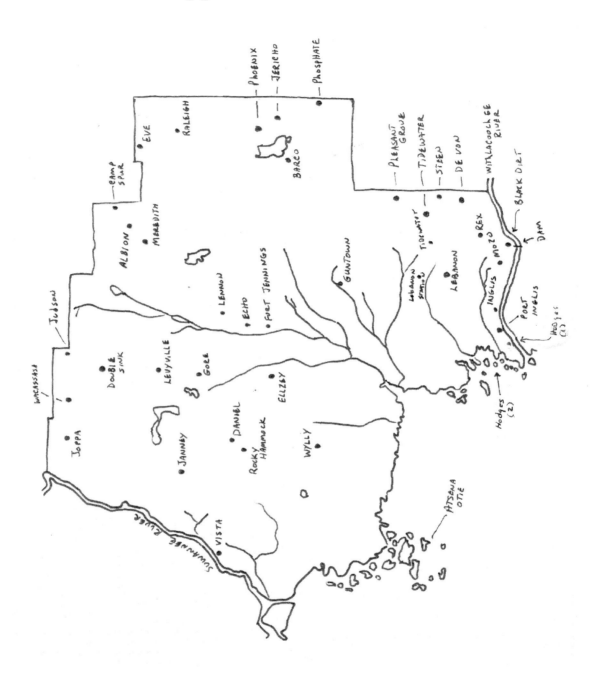

Appendix H

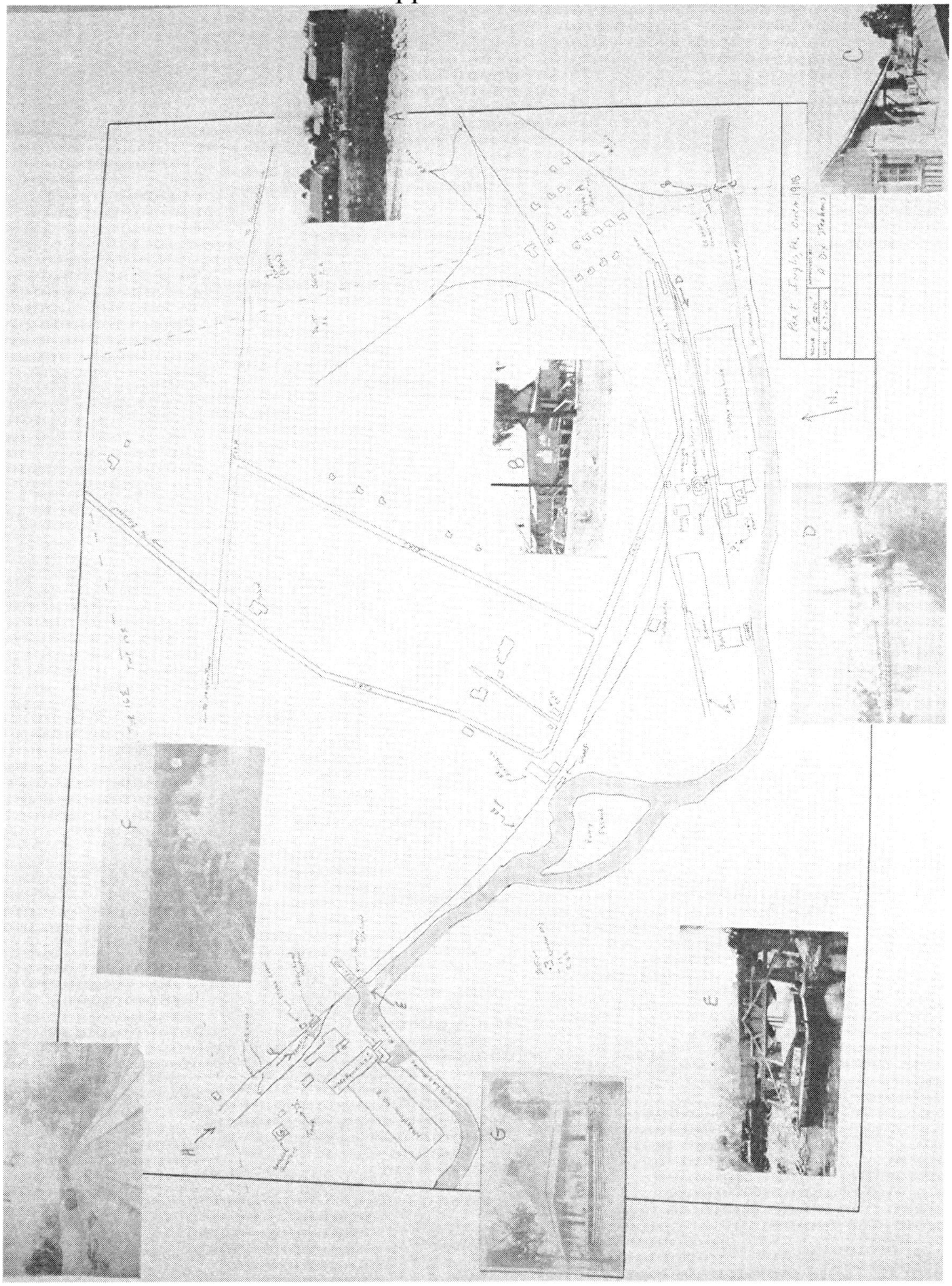

Index